Arts: A Second Level Course

The Age of Revolutions   Units 5 and 6

The Industrial Revolution

Prepared by Christopher Harvie for the Course Team

The Open University Press

The Open University Press
Walton Hall Bletchley Bucks

First published 1972
Copyright © 1972 The Open University

Designed by the Media Development Group of the Open University.

Printed in Great Britain by
EYRE AND SPOTTISWOODE LIMITED
AT GROSVENOR PRESS PORTSMOUTH

SBN 335 00562 4

This text forms part of the correspondence element of an Open University Second Level Course. The complete list of units in the course is given at the end of this text.

For general availability of supporting material referred to in this text, please write to the Director of Marketing, The Open University, Walton Hall, Bletchley, Bucks.

Further information on Open University courses may be obtained from the Admissions Office, The Open University, P.O. Box 48, Bletchley, Bucks.

INTRODUCTION

The aim of these two units and the reading associated with them is to introduce you to the study of the Industrial Revolution – why it got under way in eighteenth-century Britain, what precise industrial changes it consisted of, what effect it had on British society.

I won't attempt to spell out in detail the importance of the Industrial Revolution. You should be able to do this for yourselves in a fortnight's time. Suffice it to say that, by the end of our period, the economic part of what E. J. Hobsbawm has called the 'Dual Revolution' was becoming as important a factor in the politics of the European states as constitutional questions, while its distinctive social consequences were adding to their internal tensions.

The Industrial Revolution is a vast and complex subject, about which much is still unclear or disputed. It is not fair to you to assert a point of view as the truth where real doubt exists, so you will find many points at which our conclusions seem to be ambiguous or tentative. You will also find that many of the opinions in the two set books, E. J. Hobsbawm's *The Age of Revolution*[1] and T. S. Ashton's *The Industrial Revolution 1760–1830*,[2] are called into question by me and replaced in your mind by less firm conclusions, In fact you will find that I seem to spend time and effort in making simple things complex, in presenting two sides of a case, examining alternative methods of research, and so on.

I make no apology for this. First of all I think the first period of large-scale industrialization in Britain is fascinating enough for most of us not merely to want to know about it but how to study it ourselves. The materials to do this are readily available, objects and equipment of the time can be seen, the environment can still be experienced. While you're working on this, use your eyes on what's about you, ask questions. Would I have used this object in 1830? What would this place have looked like then? What would my work, my diet, my home, have been like then? Museums, public libraries, maps, can help here. Use them. Otherwise you may find these units tough. I have set out to *tell* you as little as possible, to get you to find out for yourself instead, by reading your set texts and making comparisons, by analysing pictorial, statistical, and verbal evidence, by studying the history of your own environment.

I have tried to simplify matters for you in Part 2 – here I want you to understand what the practical techniques were which changed industry. Although the wider economic context may need further research, or still remains a permanent subject for debate, you can, I think, master these, for they were in their time simple enough. Once you understand them, you can use this knowledge as a base from which to explore the wider field, possibly at this stage only to appreciate the difficulty of the problems posed, later on, I hope, to engage in research yourself.

A word on radio and television programmes. There is no supplement for these, they integrate into sections of the correspondence material (see Contents). Read these sections before you watch or listen. The first radio programme is concerned with the approach to our period of the late T. S. Ashton, who wrote one of the set books, *The Industrial Revolution 1760-1830*. The only television programme deals with the mechanization of the cotton textile industry which

1 Hobsbawm, E. J. (1962) *The Age of Revolution*, Mentor/New English Library Ltd.
2 Ashton, T. S. (1968) *The Industrial Revolution, 1760–1830*, Oxford University Press.

contributed to its transition from cottage to factory. The second radio programme deals with John Wilkinson, the eighteenth-century ironmaster who dramatically exemplified the factors which made for success in business at this period. You will find supplementary material to the programmes in the appropriate sections of the units.

As well as the two set texts, an essay on industrialization in eighteenth-century France is printed in the Course Reader *Revolutions 1775–1830* (F1). If you took the Arts Foundation Course you will find Unit 8 *Common Pitfalls in Historical Writing*, with the papers by E. J. Hobsbawm and R. M. Hartwell on the 'standard of living' question useful. The A100 Course Reader, *Industrialisation and Culture*[1] and the discussion of nineteenth-century industrialization in A100 Units 29–30 *The Industrialisation Process 1830–1914*, and Unit 31 *The Debate on Industrialisation*, provides additional material. Reproduced at the end of these units you will find a list of further reading; you will also find bibliographies in Ashton and Hobsbawm.

Finally, as to technique in dealing with these units. Make sure you have the *correct editions* of Ashton and Hobsbawm (Opus paperback, 1968 and Mentor paperback, 1962, respectively). Otherwise you'll have terrible trouble with my page references. Keep a bit of card handy to mask the specimen answers. You may also want to punch the course units for loose-leaf binding and interleave your notes. Whatever you do remember the three must integrate smoothly if you're to get the benefit of the course.

The assignment is printed at the beginning of the course material. I want you to look at it closely before you begin, as it will, in a sense, control the amount of work you do, section by section. You will find, when you get into Section 2, that some industries are more relevant to your own area than others. If you're pressed for time, feel free, therefore, to concentrate on these, although I think you will find it essential to work your way through Sections 2.1 (agriculture), 2.5 (textiles), 2.8 (transport), 2.9 (business organization) and 2.11 (businessmen).

---

1 Harvie, C., Martin, G., and Scharf, A. (eds.) (1970) *Industrialisation and Culture*, The Open University Press/Macmillan.

CONTENTS

In each part I will give first the overall strategic aim and then the objectives of each section, noting the role played by the TV and radio broadcasts.

Part 1

Aim

To understand the preconditions of industrial expansion in the eighteenth century, and through this the reasons why such expansion centred on the British economy.

Objectives

Section 1

To understand the divergences of opinion among reputable historians about what the Industrial Revolution was and when it started, and some of the reasons for these differences, and to understand the opposed viewpoints from which Ashton and Hobsbawm study the Industrial Revolution. (Integrated with radio programme 5, 'T. S. Ashton and the Industrial Revolution'.)

Section 2

To understand the relationship between Ashton's and Hobsbawm's ideologies and the factors they give as preconditions for industrialization. (Integrated with radio programme 5.)

Section 3

To test these 'models' of the preconditions for industrialization against aspects of the economies of eighteenth-century Britain and France.

Part 2

Aim

To grasp the nature of the technical, economic and organizational innovations which together enabled this expansion.

Objectives

To explain the technical and organizational innovations in the major industries of the period, and to show the effect of these on production, showing where interpretation of these has changed through recent research. To understand how businesses were run during the eighteenth and early nineteenth centuries. To understand how the banking system worked. To understand the combination of qualities which made for success in business. (Integrated with radio programme 6.)

Sections

1 Agriculture
2 Coal

3   Iron (integrated with radio programme 6, 'Wilkinson the Iron King')

4   The steam engine

5   Textiles (integrated with television programme 3, 'The Machine in the English Cotton Industry 1720–1820')

6   Chemicals

7   Household goods

8   Transport

9   Business organization

10   Banking

11   Businessmen

Part 3
Aim

To study the effect of industrialization on British society.

Sections

1   The landed classes, and their role in economic change.

2   The capitalists and the problem of achieving structural change in an industrial economy.

3   The working class, its well-being and the growth of its independent consciousness.

Assignment

I want you to take the area round about your own home (a square 4 miles × 4 miles with your house in the centre).

1   Draw a map of it at the present day, marking the areas you think were affected by the Industrial Revolution.

2   Detail the procedure you would take to make a study of this area in the Industrial Revolution: what questions would you ask about the area?

(The map of Bacup reproduced in Figure 1 might give you a guide to start work on. I don't want the results of your inquiry, simply the questions you would ask, the sorts of sources you would consult, and the headings under which you would deal with social and economic change in the area.) (Limit 2,000 words.)

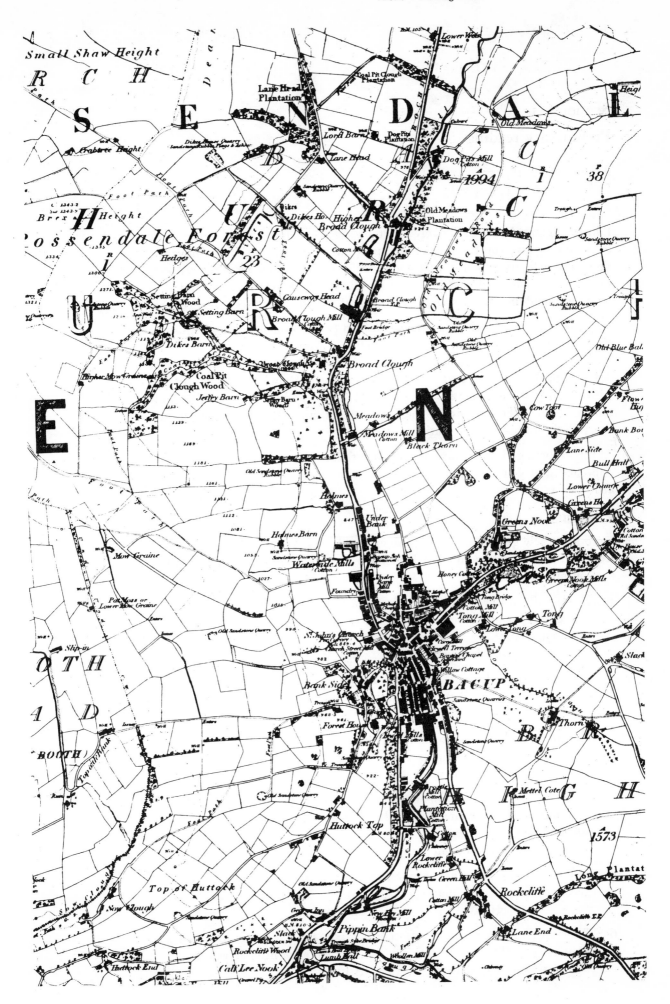

Figure 1   Bacup and district, from first edition 6″ Ordnance Survey map, 1845

PART 1

THE PRECONDITIONS OF INDUSTRIAL EXPANSION

Section 1.1

Preliminary reading

Ashton, pp. 1–18, 125–9
Hobsbawm, pp. 44–51, 72–3

I have suggested these relatively short passages for study right at the start, because they give you the drift of the approach of our writers. If you have the time and inclination, you're welcome to leaf through the whole of the set texts we're using – that's all of Ashton and Hobsbawm Chapters 2, 10, 11 and 13 – but you should find the prescribed reading at the head of each section adequate.

Now you may find it odd that I've prescribed two treatments of the Industrial Revolution, and I hope that this first section will provide a rationale for my approach. You should find, on reading through the prescribed sections of Ashton and Hobsbawm, that their interpretations differ widely. I intend here, with the help of the radio programme, 'T. S. Ashton and the Industrial Revolution' to discuss the reasons for these differences, and their relevance to the study of the Industrial Revolution.

At this early stage I don't want to ask you detailed questions about each writer's approach, but you may find the exercise below useful to 'fix' their respective attitudes to certain key developments.

EXERCISE

Here are a few general statements about the books. Your problem will be to work out which statement fits which book, by underlining in each case the appropriate author.

1   The Industrial Revolution is seen less as a single process than as a fusing of local enterprise and changes in specific industries into a huge aggregated economic change.
     Hobsbawm   Ashton

2   The treatment is logical, provided one accepts the first premises of social and economic change depending on the accumulation of one factor: capital.
     Hobsbawm   Ashton

3   The simplicity of the innovations of the period is stressed, and so the role of the innovator is not seen as a critical one.
     Hobsbawm   Ashton

4   Great stress is placed not only on technical change but on the laborious and demanding process of altering social and financial institutions to cope with industry's demands.
     Hobsbawm   Ashton

5   Cruelties and injustices are seen less as its fault, than as temporary dislocations in an improving situation.
     Hobsbawm   Ashton

6   There's a tendency to see the process as criminal rather than providential, as the creator of poverty rather than the preventer of utter starvation.
     Hobsbawm   Ashton

1	Ashton
2	Hobsbawm
3	Hobsbawm
4	Ashton
5	Ashton
6	Hobsbawm

DISCUSSION

Now I don't want to go into a general discussion of all the points raised by these questions, but at this stage, however, let's get one point straight and work out in our minds exactly what each book is trying to do.

Both are pitched at about the same level, and are attempts to synthesize and interpret existing research, subject to the fact that so much of the basic research is still going on, or has yet to be carried out. So, in a way, we can't proceed further without looking at the nature of this research in more detail. The first radio broadcast, 'T. S. Ashton and the Industrial Revolution', in fact serves as an introduction to the factors which have influenced the study of this important period of economic change.

The programme consists of a discussion between myself and five of Ashton's academic colleagues: Professors F. J. Fisher and A. H. John of the London School of Economics, Professor L. S Pressnell of the City University, and Messrs. Walter Stern and Jim Potter of L.S.E., in which we deal with Ashton's intellectual and social background, research experience, political attitudes, his work as a writer on economic history, and his ultimate achievement.

EXERCISE

Here are various questions about Ashton's activities as a historian which I want you to keep in mind during the broadcast, and subsequently answer.

1 Can you see any way in which Ashton had an 'in-built advantage' in studying the Industrial Revolution?
2 In what areas of the study of the Industrial Revolution would you expect him to be strongest, and why?
3 Look closely at Ashton pp. 77–8. This is a description of success in a steel-making concern. Do you see any hint of a moral judgement in Ashton's treatment? If so, what message do you think he is putting over?
4 Look at Ashton p. 129 and Hobsbawm pp. 72–3. Both are passages where the writers sum up their views of the whole experience. What message does Ashton seem to derive from it?
5 How does Hobsbawm contradict this?

SPECIMEN ANSWER

1 Ashton came from the Manchester area, and so could speak of the industry of this vitally important region from first-hand knowledge of its environment.
2 From the bibliography you can see that he wrote full-length books on the coal and iron industries in the Industrial Revolution; he was also a lecturer in public finance before he became a professor of economic history – which accounts for his detailed knowledge of banking and financial arrangements.
3 Ashton's implied judgement is that business success comes from hard work and thrift, and, since both imply sacrifice, the profit eventually earned is justly earned.

4   Ashton sees the self-regarding acts of the industrialists as the deliverance of Britain from a fate – of population growth without increased production – worse than the poverty attributed by other writers.

5   Hobsbawm sees the Industrial Revolution as the triumph of the bourgeoisie and their political and economic ideologies, and the worsening of the conditions of the proletariat as a consequence of this.

DISCUSSION

These five questions really highlight two major problem areas, and we will find they continually recur throughout our study.

1   When discussing the apparently straightforward 'facts' of economic and social history, we must always remember that those 'facts' are only *the facts we know about* – the 'we' being the historians who have studied the period. Historians do not, of course, 'create' their own facts, but the act of a historian approaching a subject like the rise of an industry, the career of a manufacturer, the growth of a town, expands the range of available information on that subject, as new collections of documents and other evidence and new research techniques are called into play. This is especially important in a subject like economic history, where so much of the evidence is quantifiable, so that we can, with some justification, see an advance towards a definitive account (at least of major areas of the economy). Now of course the writing of such accounts has largely taken place in no particular order, and according to no prearranged plan (although there is a greater degree of system nowadays). So that when someone like Ashton or Hobsbawm or, in a much smaller way, me, tries to write up his reading of this sort of inquiry into a general interpretation, he runs the risk of his work being patchy because of the deficiencies of these more detailed accounts. This can, of course, be compensated for by personal knowledge, but it's still a risk that writers like Ashton and Hobsbawm must run. So, as we go through these two accounts, I'll try, where it seems appropriate, to suggest where further research has confirmed or contradicted their conclusions, or otherwise altered interpretations of the Industrial Revolution.

2   Obviously an interpretation implies that a subjective attitude on the part of the historian intrudes to some extent on his treatment: that it does so is perfectly understandable. For one thing, a theory of history is always valuable for suggesting, even if only as a preliminary, possible links between various sets of facts, and evaluating their importance. You can't get away from it: if someone says he is studying 'the importance of Methodism in the Eighteenth Century' our natural reaction is to say 'importance in what context?' – which implies acceptance of a theory of religious or political or economic change at least as a basis for discussion. Secondly, economics is a science grounded on theory, but theory which is interpreted in a wide variety of ways. Out of the 'classical economics' of Adam Smith came both the defenders of the free market economy, with whom Ashton can broadly be classed, and Karl Marx's 'scientific socialism' in which tradition Hobsbawm stands. Where such differences of interpretation exist in economic and social theory, they will unquestionably exist in economic and social history.

The history of a development as relevant today as the Industrial Revolution can't be divorced from the contemporary concerns of the people who write about it. Nor should it be. The interaction of present and past has been extremely useful to the historian.

In terms of the materials of historical research, a preoccupation with contemporary industrial problems can lead to greater research into their past. During the First World War in Britain, for example, the State took control of a vast number of industries. Many business archives were for the first time opened, and when the time came to write up the record of the war effort of British industry these were widely used – frequently by historians and economists who were themselves attracted into economic history by the experience of being civil servants 'for the duration'. Again, after the Second World War, the granting of independence to the former colonial territories, and the formulation of strategies of economic development for the 'third world', caused a reawakening of interest in the economic development of eighteenth-century Britain. This came not only from British economic historians but from American economists who, challenged by the 'planned economic growth' of Soviet Russia, and its obvious attraction for the developing countries, wanted to re-examine the British experience as an example of growth promoted by 'free enterprise capitalism', and see what lessons might be derived from it.

In ways like these – and you may think of further instances as you work through these units – the preoccupations of the present day (or, at any rate, the date at which the historical treatments we rely on were written) are reflected in the study of the Industrial Revolution. As I've indicated, these can be of use to the historian in eliciting further information and giving his studies some relevance, but they also distort and tend to provide us with instances where interpretations of a given body of facts differ fundamentally. One such is the question of the 'standard of life' discussed in Part 3, where 'pessimists' like Hobsbawm clash with 'optimists' like Ashton, and of greater importance than the 'facts' in both cases would seem to be the political attitudes of both – Hobsbawm, as a socialist, being critical of capitalist industrialization, Ashton favouring it.

Such controversies have a fascination for the historian – and historians more than most academics tend to be politically engaged – but they can be rather baffling to the student. Nevertheless, we've got to appreciate the degree to which such 'political' debate enhances and distorts the problems we'll be dealing with.

Section 1.2
Historians and the Preconditions of Industrial Revolution

Preliminary reading

Ashton pp. 1–17
Hobsbawm pp. 47–57
Crouzet (the Reader, F1)

I want you to read carefully through Hobsbawm and Ashton first, and I've supplied a list of questions you will find it useful to centre your enquiry on.

1   What is the critical period when the Revolution seems to have got under way
    (a) for Hobsbawm
    (b) for Ashton?
2   Can you suggest reasons, arising from their general interpretations of the Industrial Revolution, why
    (a) Hobsbawm
    (b) Ashton
    should favour the dates they do?
3   Looking particularly at Hobsbawm, what significant additional factor does he call into play which Ashton either makes little of or considers *retarded* industrial expansion?
4   Looking particularly at Ashton, what is the special factor to which he gives prominence?

5   What relation do you think these two factors bear to the overall approaches of the two writers?

SPECIMEN ANSWER

1   For Hobsbawm the critical period comes in the 1780s, for Ashton in the 1760s.

2   Hobsbawm's reason for choosing the 1780s is that that period was when the statistics of production began to climb, and also, by implication, when Britain began to break into foreign markets (pp. 46, 52–3).

3   War: the implication of Hobsbawm's approach is, in fact, that without the enormous captive markets secured by beating down European competitors between 1793 and 1815, Britain's industrial expansion could have flopped.

4   Ashton's 'special factor' was the *rate of interest* on government stocks. [Something I'll go into in detail in Section 2.10.] A high rate inhibited industrial investment, a low rate encouraged it (p. 9).

5   Hobsbawm's view of the importance of war and colonial and semi-colonial exploitation as a vital part of the economic expansion of Britain lays stress on the ruthless use of force by British capitalism to establish its power, proving that its will to succeed generally proved greater than its fidelity to its professed reliance on free-enterprise economic theory.

Ashton's attribution of importance to the rate of interest lays stress, on the other hand, on the tension between the industrialist and the demands of government, which frequently contradicted his own plans.

DISCUSSION

Here I include discussions of both views: I leave it to you to decide which one I am discussing (underline your choice).

1   British industrialists largely got things their own way. They lived in a country which, for over a century, had been dedicated to a belief in private property and economic development, where wars both expanded industry and markets. They were no more technically knowledgeable than their continental equivalents, but they did not have to be. They had increasing supplies of capital, the freedom to use it, and markets for the taking.

Ashton   Hobsbawm

2   British industrialists had to create their institutions. It is to their credit that they did, for, although government in Britain was more sympathetic to industrial enterprise than elsewhere, many of its actions, intervention in the economy, foreign wars, were of doubtful value to industry. The Industrial Revolution was less the triumph of a particular powerful interest, than the solution of a number of complex problems in technology, economics and social and industrial organization, some of which might have proved disastrous had they not been tackled.

Ashton   Hobsbawm

SPECIMEN ANSWER

1   Hobsbawm
2   Ashton

DISCUSSION

As a Marxist, Hobsbawm interprets the preconditions for industrial revolution as the attainment by capitalism of the accumulated wealth and power necessary for it to reach its maturity. In the seventeenth century the despotic power of the monarchy was limited, and power passed to an aristocratic class which, although privileged, was prepared to extend these privileges to those prepared to buy their way into it. The 'mercantilist' policy of successive Whig governments equated strategic success with economic growth, and placed stress on the capture of markets, the creation of an effective merchant marine, and of institutions like the Bank of England (1694) which could finance these operations. At length a combination of internal prosperity (among the investing classes), extended markets and the development – fairly simple in technical terms – of an industry which enabled both factors to be effectively exploited enabled capitalist industry to advance.

EXERCISE

Now, if you were Ashton, how would you counter this explanation? I'll simplify this question by isolating three significant areas where there are opposed viewpoints.

1   Which social classes provided the impetus for industrialization?
2   Did the role of government really help industrialization?
3   Did an increase in trade and banking automatically encourage industry (see Ashton p. 81)?

SPECIMEN ANSWER

> 1   Ashton argues that economic growth was stimulated by classes which were *not* in fact possessed of political power, like the nonconformists (pp. 14–15).
> 2   Government's role was not altogether pro-industrial. The patent laws (p. 10), for instance, were probably more trouble than they were worth, and the laws against usury inhibited investment. As well as direct legislation the diversion by government of investable capital into its own funds lessened that available for industry (p. 7).
> 3   Although England had an early central banking system it was conservative in its policy towards industry, and the financial institutions which fostered trade didn't also cater for industry (p. 81).

Now, before we discuss these debatable areas, let's look at a further problem. I won't call it a precondition because, as you'll see, it doesn't quite fit the description. It concerns the role of population in industrialization.

EXERCISE

Again, I want you to look at Hobsbawm's (pp. 203–4) and Ashton's (pp. 1–6) treatment of this subject.

1   What are their interpretations of eighteenth-century population growth? How do they differ?
2   How does each influence the writer's interpretation of the role of the industrialist?

SPECIMEN ANSWER

> 1   Ashton sees population growth *preceding* industrialization, arising out of a variety of detailed reforms in hygiene, morals and so forth which *lower the death-rate* (p. 4).
>   Hobsbawm sees population growth as 'a consequence of the economic revolution rather than a precondition'.
> 2   Ashton views population growth as a *challenge* to industrialists to innovate – the alternative is poverty and starvation on an Irish scale. For Hobsbawm the rising population is a necessity of industrial society,

a mass of cheap labour to be exploited, itself substantially created by industrialism.

DISCUSSION

These are both, I must point out right away, very simplified versions of a complicated problem: the 'historical demography' of the Industrial Revolution has already become a major growth area of study, in which a wide variety of research techniques have been brought into play.

EXERCISE

From what you've read of Ashton, and from your own estimation of the problem, into what aspects of society would you research to find out about English population growth in the eighteenth century?

SPECIMEN ANSWER

From Ashton's treatment (p. 4) I would make use of:
Agricultural studies
History of clothing
History of sanitation and public health
History of science and medicine

I would also add the following:

History of individual industries
Genealogy
Statistical techniques (analyses of censuses and parish registers)
Sociological studies

DISCUSSION

The range of techniques here is obviously considerable; people from all sorts of disciplines, some quite distant from the main line of historical studies, have been drawn to this problem, attracted possibly as much by the prospect of an 'interdisciplinary study' as by the problem itself. The problem with this kind of inquiry – and this is a personal view – is that it still tends to be strongest when the individual historian is on his own stamping ground. We have only recently passed the stage of generalization and got down to the detailed studies. It will therefore be some time before generalizations founded more surely on this research will again be put forward. Those advanced by Ashton and Hobsbawm are no exception to this tendency.

This critical spirit extends as far as the 'facts' on which even the most detailed local analyses are based. There was no official census until 1801. Before then statistics of births, marriages and deaths were kept by parish priests. Can we depend on them, therefore, at a time when religious nonconformity was on the increase, when more people were moving from country parishes, where they were known to the vicar, to the towns, where there might be 20–30,000 inhabitants to a parish, when the clergy of the Church of England were notoriously lax in performing their parochial duties anyway?

Apart from this, the amount of knowledge required of the various subjects detailed above is enormous. Each subject requires, besides the particular disciplines of the historian, a professional knowledge of the subject itself. The balance of specific professional knowledge and historical judgement is a rare one to attain, and very frequently a first-rate analysis of some detailed topic in, say, medical history is confused by the writer drawing inferences from it which he does not attempt to square with other treatments because of insufficient expertise in the fields they cover.

The problem of population is a very tough nut to crack. I don't propose to add a hypothesis when I have been pointing out why a vast amount of research is needed on the subject. But I feel I must emphasize some factors which you should bear in mind when considering Ashton's and Hobsbawm's explanations.

1   I think that Ashton tends to overstate the increase in Britain's population in the first fifty years of the eighteenth century. His population rises from 5·5m. in 1700 to 6·5m. in 1750. The three estimates in Mitchell and Deane[1] give increases of 300,000, 400,000 and 200,000, a great deal lower than Ashton.

2   We have to credit the population itself with a certain dynamic of its own. The 1740s were bad years. With a high death-rate this meant that the population had the impulse to breed more, partly to make good a perceptible loss, partly because fathers died and sons succeeded them and married rather younger than they would otherwise have done. This would happen at any time of bad harvest but the rigours of the 1740s weren't repeated again. So a large young population reached breeding age just at a point when agricultural and industrial development, quite coincidentally, could sustain them. This is by and large the theory prepounded by H. J. Habakkuk in a famous article in the *Economic History Review* in 1953. It does not lay overmuch stress on an economic interpretation of population growth – a wise course in a subject so interlinked with sexual mores – but it questions the notion of early population growth as a 'challenge' to 'philanthropic' industrialists. In the imperfect state of research at the present time it convinces me most. But you must also take account of our general views on the whole subject of industrial growth before accepting what I say.

Section 1.3
Britain and France: a comparison

In addition to Ashton and Hobsbawm I have prescribed an article by the distinguished French economic historian, François Crouzet. You may already have read through it, in conjunction with Units 1 and 4, as it provides a useful economic background to the French Revolution. I may as well say that in my opinion this is one of the most convincing explanations I have seen of the requirements of the Industrial Revolution in Britain. As you can see from the complex references, it's the interpretative tip of a vast iceberg of research. Even with the reservations you ought to have about treatments of industries and regions, and generalizations from these, it's an extremely effective synthesis.

EXERCISE

(At this stage you might find it useful to make a brief précis of Crouzet's argument.)

1   To me, there is one fundamental point about the national background to industrialization made by Crouzet which is made little of by both Ashton and Hobsbawm. In your view, what is this?

2   The role of the state was pre-eminent in the economy in France between 1714 and 1789. What were the short- and the long-term effects it had on the economy according to Crouzet?

3   How does this compare with Ashton's view of the role of the state in Britain?

1 Mitchell, B. R. and Deane, P. (1962) *Abstract of British Historical Statistics*, Cambridge University Press.

4   In his treatment of the roles of war and colonial exploitation, do you think Crouzet's conclusions are nearer to Ashton's or Hobsbawm's?

5   Look at Hobsbawm on invention (p. 48). What would Crouzet's reaction be to this?

6   What is Crouzet's theory as to the critical adjustment in which England succeeded and France failed?

SPECIMEN ANSWER

1   Crouzet lays stress on the two centuries of relative peace and prosperity that preceded 1760 in Britain, giving Britain in a sense a 'flying start' in the eighteenth century – a contrast with a France embroiled in civil war in the late sixteenth and early seventeenth centuries, and thereafter subjected to an increasingly authoritarian despotism (pp. 131–2).

2   If, as Crouzet indicates, the French economy expanded as fast as, if not faster than, the British between 1714 and 1789, then the role of the state in this must have been reasonably successful. On the other hand, in the long term, state regulation was harmful in that it limited the options open to industrialists (p. 147).

3   For Ashton the role of the state was more negative: it inhibited economic activity (pp. 9–10).

4   Crouzet sees war as an important influence on economic growth, and the fact that France did badly out of the wars of the eighteenth century a reason for the slowing-up of her growth towards 1789 (pp. 155–7).

5   As a Frenchman, Crouzet denies the prominence Hobsbawm gives his country in invention, and more or less restates the traditional view of England's pre-eminence in this field (pp. 157–61).

6   Crouzet sees the critical difference between Britain and France as being that British economic and social circumstances wouldn't allow British industry simply to expand. It had to adjust its techniques as well. This factor didn't exist to the same extent in France, and the lack of avenues for individual initiative probably contributed to French technological stagnation (pp. 160–1).

DISCUSSION

What seems to me important about Crouzet's analysis is that it emphasizes the *uniqueness* of the British industrialization. Both Hobsbawm and Ashton seem to me to a great extent concerned with Britain as an *example* of industrialization. True, industrialization has subsequently been carried through in most European nations, and elements of the British experience have been inherited by later developments. But important aspects of the British experience were unique: the geography of the country, which made water-transport easy and cheap, the fortuitous combination of minerals, water supply, and climate in the areas which were to become industrial centres: the division and embarrassment of her continental rivals; the island position which assured that her wars would be fought on their territory, not hers; the fact that her aggressive foreign policy was maritime, which meant that the money spent on it didn't drain away into the expenses of an army, but maintained a fleet, with all the incidental benefits to a merchant marine that that entailed, and multiplied her colonies and markets. The French wars and British blockade of 1793–1815 accelerated this tendency by permanently damaging the maritime-based industry of France (as Crouzet has shown in another perceptive article – Crouzet, 1964).

Now this appears, by and large, to bear out Hobsbawm's theory about the role of war and colonial exploitation in establishing Britain's position. However, as you'd gather by the exercise, there is a divergence over the cause of innovation in industry: Crouzet's position is not as straightforward as Hobsbawm's. He sees no direct connection between economic growth and capital accumulation and the development of new technologies. Growth in France, 1714–89, may have been more rapid, but it was essentially a case of 'more of the same' produced in the same way from a bountiful mass of natural resources. Britain succeeded in breaking out of this position and creating new technologies less because the paths of industrialists were smooth than because they were difficult. One had to be ingenious to succeed.

Now overall I find this convincing, but it raises a lot of additional questions which we can't really settle until we've looked at the development of individual industries. Which is what we're going to be doing in Part 2.

PART 2

TECHNOLOGICAL AND ORGANIZATIONAL CHANGE IN BRITISH INDUSTRY, 1760-1830

Aim

The general aim of Part 2 is to understand the nature of the technological and organizational changes which along with economic change gave rise to the expansion of Britain's industrial output.

In Part 1 we studied in general terms the causes of the Industrial Revolution – at least in terms of the political, social and economic conditions which had to exist in Britain before the upswing in production could take place. We saw that historians' views of what these conditions were differ widely. We looked into the information and research on which those approaches were based, and I finally advanced one interpretation which I found myself more or less in agreement with, although I hope you were left sufficiently sceptical about such interpretations to realize that, pending further research, they are at best provisional.

However, there's a sense in which, at this stage, our interpretation can't be other than provisional. Until we know what the innovations in production associated with the Industrial Revolution were, and what their requirements were in terms of technological expertise, capital, labour, and organization, we can't generalize about the requirements for their exploitation on the scale of the late eighteenth century. To say this might be to imply that, in discussing the preconditions and differing interpretations of them, we have been putting the cart before the horse. My answer to this is that we need to know the general nature of the problem before we can examine detailed aspects of it, and also the less optimistic observation that such detailed studies may produce no firmer conclusions than our general discussions.

General approach

I intend to follow fairly closely the plan of Ashton's Chapter III dealing with 'The Technical Innovations' and the first half of Chapter IV dealing with 'Capital and Labour'. I will also make fairly continuous references back to Chapter II 'The Earlier Forms of Industry'.

The purpose of the correspondence material will be, in the first instance, to do two things: to simplify and demonstrate the 'machinery' of improvement – be it technical or financial – to make sure that you know what it was and how it worked, and to supplement, or where necessary criticize, Ashton's conclusions in the light of more recent research.

I have four main reasons for making this the chief part of these units.

1   I think you have to understand how a machine works and is organized along with other machines, capital, labour and managerial skills into an industrial process before you can judge how difficult the achievement was, or how easy; for that matter, whether we can properly speak of industries as being 'revolutionized' at this time.
2   We can appreciate the reality of labour conditions by examining the requirements of industry.
3   Similarly, in estimating the social impact of the Industrial Revolution, we can assess the contribution made by the mass-production of consumer goods to the standard of life.
4   We can delimit the impact of the Industrial Revolution of 1760–1830 to the developments which occurred during this period, and discriminate between these and later changes, good and bad, which we might otherwise tend to lump in with the earlier period.

EXERCISE

Before we begin, I would like you to look at the way in which Ashton (pp. 10–13 and 72–5) and Hobsbawm (p. 48) treat the process of invention in the Industrial Revolution. Below I give a short précis of the viewpoint of one of them. I want you to ascribe it to one or other of our writers (by underlining him) and then to state the objections to, or modifications of it that the other would make.

> The inventions associated with the Industrial Revolution were not the result of chance, or of individual genius; in fact they were simple and involved little theoretical knowledge: what transformed them from idea to reality was simply that the social and economic conditions now existed which enabled them to be rapidly and successfully exploited.
>   Ashton   Hobsbawm

SPECIMEN ANSWER

Hobsbawm

Ashton, on the other hand, lays stress on the need for preliminary adaptations which don't simply reflect a change in the distribution of economic power. He emphasizes the role of the *division of labour*, of *scientific advance* (pp. 10–13), the *interdependence of inventions*, the *schooling of engineers*, and the *flow of money into industry* (pp. 72–3). He also sees a transition in the type of innovation, which comes along with the supply of other factors of production to industry: the early 1700s see innovation *to increase the supply of raw material and energy;* then *to replace labour* at the mid-century; finally *to economize on capital* at the end of the century.

DISCUSSION

In all, Ashton's picture is much more complex than that of Hobsbawm. He sets the standard of actual *invention* at a higher level, and lays special stress on the process of transforming an *invention* into an *innovation* – an essential improvement to a manufacturing process.

At the end of Part 2 I will ask you again to compare the two theories in the light of the studies of individual industries which now follow.

Section 2.1
Agricultural Improvement

Preliminary reading

Ashton pp. 18–22 and 48–52
Hobsbawm pp. 49, 67–70
(*Industrialisation and Culture* C6, F1)

I want you to begin by noting down Hobsbawm's view of the main functions of agriculture in an industrializing society.

SPECIMEN ANSWER

1 By rising productivity, to support a growing non-agricultural population.
2 To provide recruits for factory industry and town population.
3 To provide capital for the growth areas of the economy.
4 Creating a market among the mass of the agricultural population.
5 Providing an export surplus to pay for imports of capital for modern industry.

This gives us a fairly straightforward interpretation of the course of agricultural change, which integrates it closely with parallel changes in industrial organization. But before we discuss in detail how credible an explanation it is, I'd like you to go through the pages in Ashton which deal with agricultural change (look also at pp. 85–6 and 116–8) and, *taking Hobsbawm's list*, check whether Ashton agrees or disagrees with him on each function ascribed to agricultural change.

Now in general, between Ashton and Hobsbawm, is there:

(a) a total disagreement about both what happened and whether it was beneficial;
(b) an agreement as to what happened, but divergent judgements about it;
(c) full agreement about both matters?

SPECIMEN ANSWER

1 By and large, Ashton agrees (p. 49).
2 Ashton doesn't agree totally: he argues that (a) there was no agricultural depopulation and (b) that where migration occurred it occurred because of increased opportunity in the towns rather than because of a compulsion to leave the land (p. 50).
3 Ashton doesn't deal with this directly in his section on agriculture, but when he deals with banking on pp. 85–6 he argues that the profits of farming were made available through banks to industrialists who wanted to borrow.

4 and 5   are largely discounted by Hobsbawm himself in the British context, and Ashton doesn't allude much to them either, but on pp. 116–8 he makes the point that a bad harvest could still mean a decline in industrial investment.

My choice would be:
(b) an agreement as to what happened, but divergent judgements about it.

What Hobsbawm sees as being inevitable and unpleasant (like the whole industrialization process itself, with the same victims and villains), Ashton sees as inevitable and, by and large, an improvement for all concerned.

DISCUSSION

We have become quite familiar with this sort of disagreement between Ashton, the apologist for capitalist industry, and Hobsbawm, the Marxist critic. Their judgements largely hinge on the vexed standard of living question and, by and large, are conditioned by the general view they take of the consequences of the economic change in general.

EXERCISE

For instance, imagine that Ashton and Hobsbawm were confronted with evidence that, in a certain parish, poverty had increased in the 1820s and 1830s. What would be the general explanation and reaction of (a) Ashton (see also pp. 88–9) and (b) Hobsbawm?

SPECIMEN ANSWER

(a)   Ashton
would tend to attribute this to the imperfect working of the capitalist system – for instance the persistence of the Old Poor Law, which nineteenth-century liberal politicans believed encouraged pauperism by its readily available poor relief, and discouraged moves to industrial areas.

(b)   Hobsbawm
would attribute it to the desire of capitalists to drive labour from under-employment in the country to town and factory employment by making things more difficult for the country poor.

DISCUSSION

Given this sort of disagreement, we are naturally driven back to look at the sort of sources historians like Ashton and Hobsbawm rely on, in other words to a more specialized study of agricultural history.

EXERCISE

1   I want you to look over Ashton pp. 49–52, and his bibliography, and note below the sorts of evidence you think Ashton used in writing his account.
2   Now bearing in mind our discussion (Section 1.2) of the nature of recent research into our period, I want you to suggest where further progress is likely to be made in investigation of agricultural change, and what means are likely to be used to make it public.

SPECIMEN ANSWER

Bills and Acts of Parliament, Petitions
Contemporary writers on agriculture, cf Arthur Young
Standard historical writings on the subject, cf Lord Ernle's *English Farming Past and Present*
Census and taxation returns
Farm equipment
Contemporary periodicals cf *Farmer's Magazine* and proceedings of contemporary 'improving' groups and individuals
Reports of the Board of Agriculture
Learned articles by present day researchers

The main accession to our knowledge about this problem is most likely to come through increasing research into agricultural change either on a local basis or in terms of one type of agriculture, i.e. stock rearing. This research is most likely to be transmitted by theses and learned articles.

DISCUSSION

The earlier historians of the Industrial Revolution by and large drew on an accessible but narrow range of sources. Documents like Parliamentary Reports and the accounts of contemporary commentators are of course valuable, but they tend to focus attention on remarkable instances of progress or particularly bad black spots, rather than on the 'normal' situation. So both the 'optimist' and the 'pessimist' can continue to derive comforting conclusions from them, without really assisting the extension of our knowledge of the problem.

Here, as elsewhere, the area of advance has become that of detailed research based on estate records, local accounts, population statistics, maps, and a study of farm architecture and equipment. Some of this research might deal with localities, some with particular types of cultivation or farm ownership, with land laws or estate management, or with aspects of the connections which existed between agriculture and industry.

EXERCISE

(A)   Below you will find definitions of, or examples of, certain phenomena we associate with agricultural improvement.[1] I want you to note the accepted historical term for each phenomenon described or exemplified, and describe the role it played in agrarian improvement.

Figure 2

1 (2) is from the *Oxford English Dictionary*; (3) and (6) are quoted from *New Statistical Account of Scotland: Roxburghshire*. 1845, pp. 329 and 403.

2   'The settlement of the succession of a landed estate, so that it cannot be bequeathed at pleasure by any one possessor.'

3   'The system is that of the four and five-shift courses, the former predominating. Turnips or potatoes are taken as a fallow-crop; this is followed by wheat or barley, sown down with grass-seeds; and when these grasses are taken up at the end of one or two years an oat crop follows; no manure being applied to any but the turnip crop.'

4

Figure 3

5

Figure 4

6   'In 1826 a market for cattle and horses, at the recommendation of the Club, was established at Hawick on the May fair-day, and the Club in that year paid £8 towards defraying the expense of a young man attending Mr. Dick's Veterinary Lectures in Edinburgh, on condition of his settling as a farrier in Hawick.'

(B)   Now here are two maps: Figure 5 shows the boundary of the main areas of British agriculture, and identifies the main crops grown and livestock reared. I leave you to identify what the areas in Figure 6 represent (answer in notebook).

You will also notice several letters in Figure 6. Each of the situations in the left-hand column corresponds to one of them. I want you to 'match' each, by circling the appropriate letter.

An expanding population of small tenant farmers   a b c d e

An area of high wages caused by the existence of local
factory employment   a b c d e

An area of poorly-paid landless labourers   a b c d e

An area of 'old' enclosure   a b c d e

An area of market-gardening   a b c d e

Main Areas of Agriculture

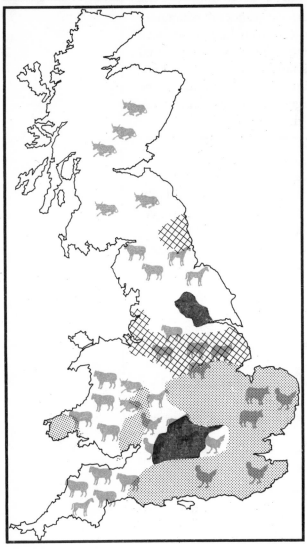

Figure 5

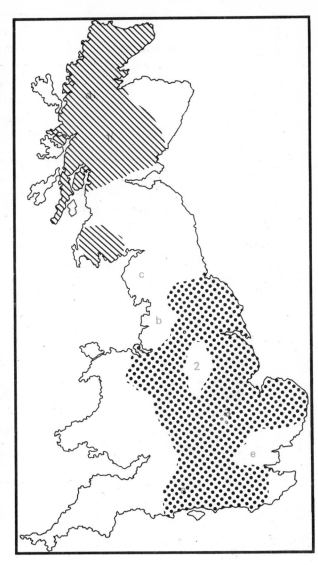

Figure 6

	Barley		Wheat
	Lean Cattle		Oats
	Fat Cattle		Poultry
	Horses		Sheep

SPECIMEN ANSWER

A

1 a common-field village	2 entail
This inhibited development because holdings were scattered and there was much wasteland. Agreement between the various tenants was also difficult.	Entail was a system of mortgaging the land by settling it (usually on the eldest son) and raising money on its security (sometimes for agricultural improvement).

3 crop-rotation	4 enclosed village
This enabled the raising of two feeding crops (turnips and grasses) which also enriched the soil for the two cereal crops.	The various grades of commoner tenants and freeholders have been converted into large tenants and landless labourers. Waste has been taken into cultivation and on the new large fields a rotation is being practised.

5 prize bull	6 an agricultural society
Before the mid-eighteenth century cattle were usually small and were sold off for fattening annually or just killed. Better stockbreeding, and of course, winter feed crops, enabled heavier beasts to be bred and kept.	These were forums where landowners with an interest in improvement could exchange information; they also organized shows and competitions which stimulated innovation.

B

> 1   Represents the peasant-farming areas of the north of Scotland and Ireland.
> 2   Represents areas largely occupied in sheep-rearing and long since enclosed.
> 3   Represents the arable area affected by the enclosures of the eighteenth and nineteenth centuries.

An expanding population of small tenant farmers	a b c (d) e
An area of high wages caused by the existence of local factory employment	a (b) c d e
An area of poorly-paid landless labourers	(a) b c d e
An area of 'old' enclosure	a b (c) d e
An area of market-gardening	a b c d (e)

DISCUSSION

Hobsbawm describes (p. 68) such changes and improvements as small ones which had a disproportionately large impact simply on account of the general inefficiency of British agriculture. Both he and Ashton (p. 52) are agreed in seeing the combination of a fully rationalized system of organization and the adoption of 'scientific' methods and machinery as coming late in the day. In the following paragraph Hobsbawm makes the point that the politics of the semi-reformed 'agricultural interest', were really a sort of protest against industry. But after all, the society which had traditionally controlled local government and, until 1868, parliamentary government was an agrarian-based one, in which the relations between landlord and tenant and local merchants had a political as well as an economic aspect. The great houses continued the greatest influences on the church and the army and, as you'll see in Section 3.1, they had close relations with commerce and manufacture as well.

EXERCISE

However, after 1830 agriculture definitely becomes more of an *industry* and less of an *interest*. And, apart from the political and economic changes we have been dealing with, the reason was one of technical change. From what you've read about advances of technology in general during the Industrial Revolution period, I want you to note down four direct effects improved technology might be expected to have on farming by 1830.

SPECIMEN ANSWER

1   The growth of the chemical industry meant the greater use of simple chemicals – notably lime – in agriculture.
2   Better transport meant such aids were more cheaply available and that marketing was easier.
3   Plentiful supplies of iron and steel meant better and more durable equipment.
4   The steam engine was coming into use both for drainage and as a light power-unit for farm work.

DISCUSSION

Such developments really lie at the very end of our period, but the foundation for them was being laid by the economic and social adjustments of the eighteenth century and the rudimentary application of scientific techniques.

All this time, however, British agriculture was shielded from foreign competition by high protective tariffs. When these came off in the 1840s the organizational head-start it had gained enabled it for upwards of two decades to withstand foreign competition, but by the 1870s it was crushed by the effect of the mechanized production and conveyance of crops from abroad. However, this was merely a further stage in the rationalization of agriculture from interest to industry. The bits that did well ministered directly to the needs of industrial Britain – market gardening, dairy produce – while the inhabitants of the industrial towns benefited from the import of cheap grain and meat.

Recent research into agriculture at the time of the Industrial Revolution has tended to modify our traditional picture of its role. The general tendency has been to see a continuity of change in organization and ownership at least from the period of the Restoration, when the tensions associated with the social changes of the Reformation were settled in the interests of the country gentlemen of moderate estates. From these came improvements in stock-rearing and arable farming which were, by the mid-eighteenth century, lowering the price of food and so liberating funds throughout society for the purchase of manufactured goods.

Section 2.2
The Coal Industry

Preliminary reading

Ashton pp. 26–30, 53
(*Industrialisation and Culture* F4, 5, 6)

The objectives of this section are relatively straightforward ones because Ashton's treatment of the coal industry in *The Industrial Revolution 1760–1830*, is essentially a drastically condensed version of his extended work *The Coal Industry of the Eighteenth Century* which he first published in 1929.[1] We discussed right at the beginning the pitfalls of writing general textbooks about a controversial period like this, and the difficulty of relating wide treatment with

---

1 Ashton, T. S. and Sykes, J. (1964) *The Coal Industry of the Eighteenth Century*, 2nd revised edition, Manchester University Press.

detailed research. Here Ashton, however, is pretty secure, as he himself had done the basic groundwork.

Nevertheless, in his anxiety to provide a concise treatment of the subject, Ashton uses technical terms and descriptions of equipment which you may find it difficult to grasp the meaning or use of.

EXERCISE

I am going to give you a reconstruction of an eighteenth-century colliery. From the descriptions given in Ashton I want you to identify various items of equipment illustrated in the drawing. You will find various numbered items of equipment *in* the drawing. In the numbered boxes on the right-hand side I want you to enter the description.

Then in the margin note down what area of Britain you think the colliery might be in, what period the drawing represents, and why.

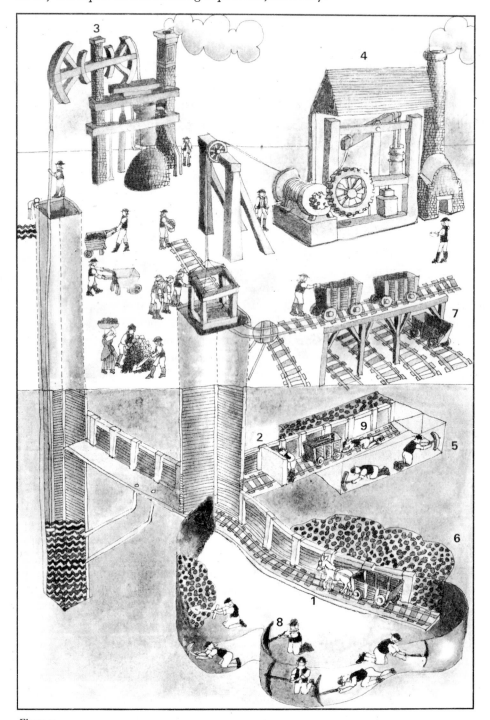

Figure 7

SPECIMEN ANSWER

1	underground waggon way, pit-pony and truck
2	brattice
3	atmospheric pumping engine
4	steam winding engine
5	longwall face
6	goaf
7	surface waggon ways
8	hewer
9	putter

This colliery is in the Midlands because of the longwall working. The date of the picture is about 1800 because of the use of the steam winding engine. As you can see, it represents a fairly advanced coal mine of the sort reasonably common by the end of the century.

What Ashton says about the nineteenth century really being the age of coal is borne out by this table of production (Mitchell and Deane, *op. cit.*).

Coal Production, 1700-1900

1700	2·5	million tons
1750	4·75	million tons
1800	10	million tons
1829	16	million tons
1854*	64·7	million tons
1875	133·3	million tons
1900	225·2	million tons

*official statistics begin

EXERCISE

Suggest two reasons for this advance.

SPECIMEN ANSWER

1 The increased use of the steam engine instead of the water-wheel in manufacturing industry.
2 The growth of the steam-operated railway system from the 1830s on, stimulating demand for coal and metal products.

DISCUSSION

You might have included improvements in coal extraction, but in fact such improvements did not make a very large impact. Mechanical coal-cutters were experimented with from the beginning of the nineteenth century, but technical success was not achieved until the 1860s, and in fact such machinery did not cut more than fifty per cent until 1935. One important transition was, however, achieved by the 1830s. Because of improvements in the conveyance of coal from the face to the surface, by the use of ponies, trams and rails, the proportion of hewers to other operatives changed from roughly 1:3 in 1700 to 2:1 in 1800. Productivity increased because of this, but bottlenecks remained, substantially because demand was not increasing dramatically enough to force their elimination.

27

What in fact was the demand for coal composed of? Well, let's look at two breakdowns of the destination of coal mined (Figure 8). On the top is Dr. Baron Duckham's[1] calculation of the output and consumption of Scottish coal in 1800; on the bottom is a breakdown of coal production and consumption in 1913 (from Mitchell and Deane, *op. cit.*).

EXERCISE

What is the major difference you notice between the two breakdowns?

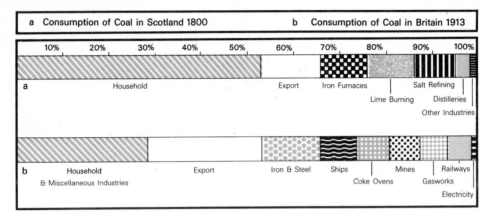

Figure 8

SPECIMEN ANSWER

> Domestic consumption has (proportionately) fallen: industrial consumption has increased.

DISCUSSION

What we can gather from this is that even the 'growth area' of coal consumption – chemicals, the cotton industry, even the iron industry – was, in 1800, only a tiny fraction of the domestic demand. This was fairly dramatically demonstrated by the great export of coal from the Northumberland and Durham coalfield to London.

Nevertheless by 1800 the industrial consumption sector, though small, was growing rapidly. More significantly the use of coal was becoming an integral part of the technologies of other industries, as a substitute for other fuels, raw materials, and sources of power, and as an essential part of new industries, like chemicals.

EXERCISE

Finally, one particular bottleneck was to lead to a remarkable advance right at the end of our period. What do you think it was? (Turn to Section 2.8.)

Section 2.3
The Iron Industry

Preliminary reading
Ashton pp. 30–4, 53–5

Introduction

Again, we can put a great deal of confidence in Ashton's version, as he wrote, (1924) an extended treatment, *Iron and Steel in the Industrial Revolution*,[2] which

---

1 Duckham, Baron F. (1970) *A History of the Scottish Coal Industry*, David and Charles, p. 28.

2 Ashton, T. S. (1963) *Iron and Steel in the Industrial Revolution*, 3rd revised edition, Manchester University Press.

he based substantially on the papers of Midlands industrialists, and which includes an extended study of the career of John Wilkinson, who figures in our second radio broadcast. So to some extent this section acts as a supplement (along with Section 2.11) to the broadcast.

First of all, I want to go through the improvements in the productive process. I am going to start by giving you a drawing of the more important stages about 1820. I want you to identify each stage and note where significant advances were achieved after about 1700.

Figure 9

SPECIMEN ANSWER

1 coke blast furnace	2 blowing engine	3 reverberatory remelting furnace for puddling	4 rolling and slitting mill
Introduced by Abram Darby at Coalbrookdale, 1709, replacing charcoal furnaces. In general use by 1750s.	The steam engine was adapted to blowing furnaces by 1780 in Staffordshire.	'Puddling' was invented to remove impurities from cast iron smelted in coke furnaces preparatory to forging, by Henry Cort, 1783.	Rolling was also introduced by Cort, though slitting into bars was traditionally done by water-powered mills.

DISCUSSION

Why did coke-smelting (1) take so long to catch on?

Well, it was partly because of chemical differences between types of coal found on the various coalfields, and partly because the scarcity of fuel referred to by Ashton may not in fact have existed, as the sort of wood used to make charcoal is quite different from that needed to build ships. (Shiptimbers came from fully-grown trees, while charcoal wood came from saplings.)

EXERCISE

Now look at this map of ironworks established in Scotland between 1700 and 1800.

1 Ring the ironworks which used charcoal for smelting.   1 2 3 4 5 6 7 8 9 10

2 The ironworks which used coal for smelting.   1 2 3 4 5 6 7 8 9 10

3 Can you suggest a reason for the founding of ironworks 3 and 4?

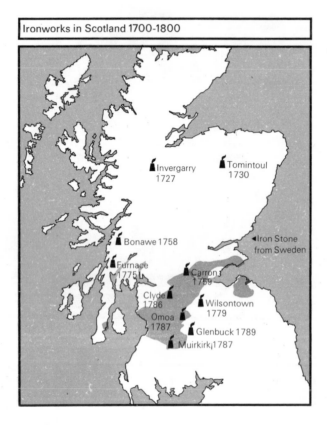

Ironworks in Scotland 1700-1800

Figure 10

SPECIMEN ANSWER

1	Charcoal-using ironworks.	(1) (2) (3) 4 (5) 6 7 8 9 10
2	Coal-using ironworks.	1 2 3 (4) 5 (6) (7) (8) (9) (10)

3 Ironworks 3 and 4 were founded between 1757–63, a period during which Britain was engaged in the Seven Years War.

DISCUSSION

War had an extremely important effect in stimulating the expansion of iron-manufacturing and general metalworking in Britain. One of the best ways of calculating its impact is to think about the sort of equipment eighteenth-century wars needed. I imagine you know pretty well what the ships and military equipment of the period looked like – look through the various illustrations in Hobsbawm if you don't.

EXERCISE

A   Note down where you think iron would be used in (a) cast and (b) wrought form, and (c) where other metals might be used.

B   From the broadcast on the Wilkinsons, can you suggest two effects war had on iron making, one bad and one good?

SPECIMEN ANSWER

A Cast iron would be used for cannon and shot on land and sea, wrought iron for nails and mast-hoops at sea, light arms, horse-shoes and wheel-types on land. Steel would be used for swords and bayonets, brass for harness and buckles, and copper for sheathing hulls.

B 1 Bad   Expansion of capacity to cope with armaments orders could lead to a slump following their withdrawal when peace came.

2 Good   Technological innovations spurred on by war – i.e. Wilkinson's cannon-boring process – could be adapted to peacetime uses.

DISCUSSION

As you would gather from Ashton's remarks on p. 126, he saw war essentially as a *discontinuity* in economic progress. However this view has now been challenged, especially, as you might gather, in the case of the metal industries. War both *stimulated demand* and *restricted imports*, driving English entrepreneurs to innovate in order to utilize available resources. When the demand generated by war receded, such newly created excess capacity could be transferred to stimulating a new domestic demand – for instance Coalbrookdale Ironworks used spare pig iron to cast rails for the works' waggonways, the first widespread use of iron rails in Britain. This capacity in due course supplied a vast range of equipment for civil use.

EXERCISE

I want you to look closely at (a) Figure 54, the Euston Arch, in Hobsbawm, and (b) the drawing of a working-class interior below. I want you to tackle them in the same way as you tackled the previous question, allocating the metal items to their various descriptions.

Figure 11

SPECIMEN ANSWER

	cast	wrought	other metals
(a)	railings, lamp-standards	wheel-tyres, horse-shoes, hinges	*brass:* horse-brasses, buttons
(b)	oven and firegrate, pots	chains and fire irons	*steel:* cutlery

DISCUSSION

'Domestic' items like these were produced in increasing quantities after the 1760s. Following the construction of the Coalbrookdale iron bridge in 1779, cast iron was used for an increasing variety of civil engineering projects, as well as for urban decoration – fanlights and window-frames as well as railings – and in the skeleton-construction of factories and warehouses.

The production of small castings – pots and pans (called 'hollow-ware'), cast-iron ovens and firegrates – had an impact throughout the country by the middle of the century. Other metal goods – stamped brassware, buttons and candlesticks, small arms – followed them on to the coalfields, as they needed a greater weight of fuel than of metal. The Birmingham region was of major importance, combining traditional skills, accessible minerals, and a central position. Its workshops were small concerns, but one in particular, that of Matthew Boulton, reached considerable dimensions and applied power to the production of a wide range of domestic utensils and armaments. However, it was shortly to make power its business, as the local scarcity of water-power drove Boulton, with his partner James Watt, to experiment with steam power, and then to monopolize it.

The role of steam-power in the metal industries should not, however be over-estimated. Ashton credits steam with a considerable influence, but we must note that the burden of his research was concentrated on the West Midlands. Admittedly this was a major area for metal production, but by the early years of the nineteenth century production was rising more rapidly in Scotland and South Wales, and what evidence exists doesn't indicate any great use of steam engines there. Probably this was because geography and climate made the use of water-power in these areas a more attractive prospect than in the relatively arid West Midlands.

Steel

What about steel? We use steel nowadays for such a wide range of items – from cutlery to structural engineering – that we can only really understand its role in the Industrial Revolution when we grasp the fact that its range of uses then was tiny, virtually limited to weapons, scissors, cutlery, and springs for clockmaking. This was substantially because of the complexity of the manufacturing process. Even Ashton's lucid exposition might baffle you, so I've drawn up a diagrammatic treatment of its manufacture.

Manufacture was concentrated around Sheffield, where a generous supply of water-power was provided by the streams pouring off the Pennines. Steel production grew steadily throughout our period, with substantial increases in time of war, but quantitative advance had to wait until the Bessemer, Siemens and Gilchrist-Thomas processes revolutionized production in the mid and late nineteenth century.

Steel Manufacture after the Invention of the Crucible Process

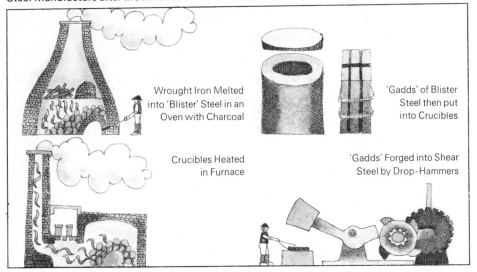

Wrought Iron Melted into 'Blister' Steel in an Oven with Charcoal

'Gadds' of Blister Steel then put into Crucibles

Crucibles Heated in Furnace

'Gadds' Forged into Shear Steel by Drop-Hammers

Figure 12

Section 2.4
The Steam Engine

Preliminary reading
Ashton pp. 28–30 and 55–8
(*Industrialisation and Culture* CI)

EXERCISE

Below you will find two sets of three pictures. Each set illustrates the phases of operation of the Newcomen and the Watt type of engine, although it's up to you to find out which is which.

I want you to do this by describing in your notebook the movements made by the engine at each phase of operation.

1   Which engine is represented in
     diagram 1
     diagram 2?
   Which is the more efficient engine, and why?

Diagram 1 (Figure 13)
(a) (b)

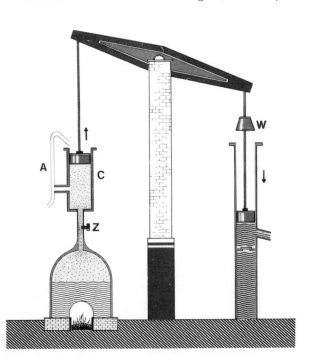

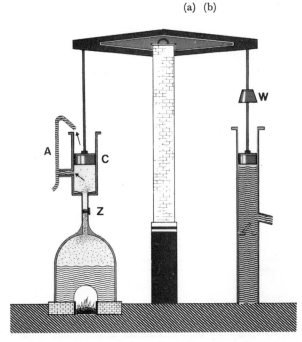

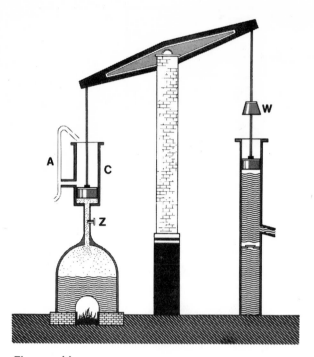

Figure 13 (c)

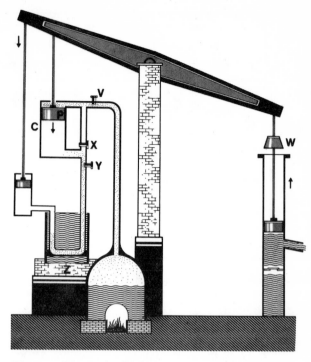

Diagram 2 (Figure 14)   (a)

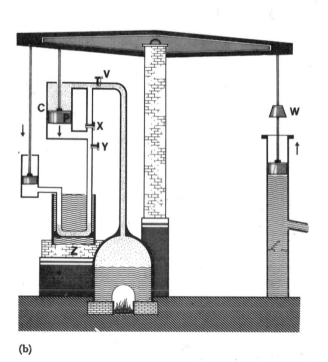

(b)

(c)

SPECIMEN ANSWER

1(a) While the weight, W, is pushing the column of water down it raises the piston. Steam at a very low pressure is being admitted to cylinder C through open valve Z.

1(b) Valve Z is closed. The cylinder is cooled by jets of water A, which causes the steam inside it to condense, creating a 'vacuum'. This pulls the piston down, and raises water in the pump.

1(c) Valve Z is opened. The vacuum is destroyed, so W can begin to push the water down again.

2(a) The weight W has descended. Steam is entering the top of the cylinder C under low pressure through valve V. A vacuum is being created in the lower part of the cylinder by steam condensing in the condenser Z through Valve Y.

2(b) The piston P descends into this vacuum, pulling W up.

2(c) The valve Y is now closed, the valve X opened, which means pressure is now equal on both sides of the piston, which rises as weight W falls.

1 is the Newcomen engine, 2 is the Watt engine.

The more efficient engine is the Watt, as the condenser, not the cylinder, is cooled to provide the vacuum. When condensing goes on in the cylinder, then it has to be cool. But to receive steam it must be hot. So in the Newcomen engine a lot of energy was expended in repeatedly reheating the cylinder. Watt's engine dispensed with this.

DISCUSSION

The increase in efficiency caused by Watt's improvements is easily seen when we consider that Newcomen's original engine took 32 lbs. of coal to generate one horse power while Watt's took only 9 lbs. He was not the only engineer wanting to modify the atmospheric engine. John Smeaton, the civil engineer, carried out several detailed improvements to the type after 1772 which halved its fuel consumption. It could be argued that Watt's innovation was so simple that its adoption was only a matter of time, but if we thought that we would miss a very important factor in the technology of the eighteenth century: the fact that engineers like Watt had no standards of performance to judge by. The atmospheric engine might look ludicrously inefficient by our standards, but it was the best its day had, and for the fifty or so years it was in operation in British collieries and waterworks, few thought it could be improved on.·

EXERCISE

In this situation what 'scientific' advantage had Watt?

SPECIMEN ANSWER

Watt had access to the theoretical evaluations of the efficiency of atmospheric engines being made at Glasgow University.

DISCUSSION

This factor is significant. The steam engine was the most sophisticated product of the Industrial Revolution – certainly as far as Britain was concerned. Its technical development had always been closely tied up with scientific advance, especially with research into the properties of vacuums. Research into this had been carried on in the universities of the continent in the seventeenth century, and in 1700 Thomas Savery demonstrated his mine-pump before the

Royal Society. Once the atmospheric engine was proved a practical possibility there was a lapse in theoretical discussion, however, until Watt's experiments in the 1760s in Glasgow, a town with a university which had a reputation for scientific research. Indeed, it's difficult to see where else such an advance could have come from in Britain, with scientific scholarship at Oxford and Cambridge at a low ebb (see Ashton p. 15).

I think we can say therefore that the scientific basis of Watt's advance – the comparing of the practical operation of the Newcomen engine with its theoretical possibilities – owed much to Watt's university connections. However, the development of a prototype and the numerous problems to be overcome called for a different environment, that of the well-established engineering works of Matthew Boulton in Birmingham, who could afford the expenses involved, which Watt estimated at £13,000 when he applied for an extension of his patent in 1775.

Watt and his patent

I want to look briefly at this stage at the part played by patents in the Industrial Revolution, using Watt's case as an illustration. First I want you to note down the main points Ashton makes in his discussion of patents (p. 10) for and against the practice.

SPECIMEN ANSWER

> For
> Patents gave security to the inventor.

> Against
> They could enable an inventor to stop other inventors improving or modifying his work; both maintaining him in a privileged position and inhibiting progress.

DISCUSSION

Ashton's final position is non-committal: 'It is at least possible that without the apparatus of the patent system discovery might have developed quite as rapidly as it did.' It's difficult not to agree with him: if there was abuse on one side, there were cases, on the other, of inventors like Crompton who, because their machines were not patented, did not prosper, and so were not able to make further innovations.

Watt's monopoly was conservative in some respects: he opposed the use of steam at high pressure *driving* the piston with its expansive force rather than *sucking* it along by condensing, and in so doing set his face against the development of the high-pressure steam engine which was, in locomotive form, to be of immense importance in the nineteenth century. He opposed the 'compound' engine, in which steam passed through two cylinders, at high pressure in one and at low pressure in the other, which was also to become important later on, especially at sea.

But his opposition was not totally wrong-headed: his main desire was to see the steam engine (and the fortunes of Boulton and Watt) securely established, and he opposed developments which seemed to go too far and too fast. High-pressure steam involved the danger of boiler explosions, such explosions could imperil, in a process of 'guilt by association', the whole future of the steam engine. On the other hand he was quick to explore ways which increased the efficiency and utility of his own engine. Ashton notes three of his further inventions on p. 57. These were:

Figure 15

The sun and planet motion (1781) which enabled the up-down motion of the pump-rod to drive a flywheel round by means of the fixed cog A rotating round the rim of the hub-cog of the flywheel B.

The parallel motion (1784) which guided the upper end P of the piston-rod up and down.

The centrifugal governor (1788) – this consisted of two balanced rotating weights Z attached by a band K to the flywheel: as the flywheel rotated faster, centrifugal force drove the weights further apart, and this movement in its turn controlled a valve G supplying steam to the cylinder.

Now these were rather akin to the various processes associated with spinning patented by Arkwright. They consolidated a major *invention* and made it into an applicable process. The rotary motion made the steam engine an alternative motive force to the water-wheel, while the governor, in particular, made it a much more sensitive and regular source of motive power than its water-wheel competitor. Ultimately the fact that over four hundred engines were installed within only twenty years is the best proof of the success of Watt's policy.

The use of the steam engine

Now Ashton makes a fairly bold claim for the steam engine. It was 'the pivot on which industry swung into the modern age'. Certainly, the view traditionally held of the Industrial Revolution was more or less this. Arnold Toynbee wrote in 1882:

> In 1785 Boulton and Watt made an engine for a cotton-mill at Papplewick in Notts, and in the same year Arkwright's patent expired. These two facts taken together mark the introduction of the factory system.

As you can infer from our discussion in the introduction to these units, there has been a general drift away from standpoints as explicit as this, and one factor which has been, and is being, subjected to a critical reappraisal is the role of the steam engine.

Because of the steam engine's later spectacular history, there was a general tendency to see it as the major motive-force of the first Industrial Revolution and to underplay, or even forget about, the part played by pre-existent forms of motive power. This tendency has been checked from the 1920s of this century on, with a growing number of publications on its technical and economic history.

EXERCISE

Suggest two possible approaches to estimating the influence of the steam engine in British industry *c.* 1800.

SPECIMEN ANSWER

> 1   You can look at the question through the records engine makers kept of the engines they built and where they went.

> 2   You can study it from the standpoint of the industries in which they were used and their influence in these industries.

DISCUSSION

Now up to 1800 the approach appears relatively simple: since Boulton and Watt held the patent for steam engines they had a monopoly of their installation.

So from their records it should be possible to construct a picture of the use of engines up to 1800. This, in fact, was what John Lord did (Lord, 1930). Unfortunately, the record is less than accurate, as some 'pirate' building of engines went on, whose records did not, of course, pass to Boulton and Watt. Still, I've abstracted from Mr. Lord's list of the industries for which Boulton and Watt built engines, the total number and horsepower of the six biggest users.

Industry	Engines installed by 1800	
	No.	H.P.
Cotton Mills	84	1382
Foundries and Forges	28	618
Copper Mines	22	440
Collieries	30	380
Canals	18	261
Water Works	13	241

Now this shows that cotton mills were obviously important buyers of steam engines. But if you wanted to compare the impact of steam-power with water-power in *the cotton industry*, how would you go about it?

SPECIMEN ANSWER

> Try to estimate the horsepower of water-wheels working in the industry at a given date and compare it with the horsepower of steam engines at the same date.

DISCUSSION

Obviously a pretty tall order, as a huge amount of research is necessary to establish the number of, say, cotton factories in operation at any given time. Such intensified local research is of relatively recent origin, and much more will have to be done before we can safely generalize about the impact of the steam engine. If four horsepower was generated by steam engines to every one generated by water-wheel in the cotton industry in 1838, we still don't know how recent this development was.

Local research seems to indicate, however, that the steam engine came relatively late to most British industry. Like the motor car at the beginning of the twentieth century, it needed specialized maintenance, and until this was available its development was limited. I think it would be right to see the breakthrough taking place from the 1820s on, when fully automatic spinning machinery and power-looms became a practical possibility, and the economic boom of the mid-1820s brought about an increase in factory building.

Always remember the large size water-wheels could attain. The largest steam engine Boulton and Watt built by 1800 generated about 80 h.p. while contemporary water-wheels could manage up to 150 h.p.

Always remember, too, the distinction between the 'low-pressure' engines of Watt and the 'high-pressure' engines of Trevithick (see A100 Units 29–30, Section 1.4, and Hobsbawm, Figure 80 'The Rocket'). The latter, using a pressure of forty or fifty pounds to the square inch, were used as portable engines and as the first locomotives. None could be considered to have superseded the others; at the end of our period all – including atmospheric engines – were in use in their various fields. But the most dramatic future role was assigned to the high-pressure engine.

Section 2.5
Innovation in the textile industry

Introduction

This section will largely act as an extended supplement to television programme 3 '*The Machine in the English Cotton Industry*'. Those of you who have been able to see the programme will find it relatively straightforward; if you haven't, you'll find its method more roundabout, but I have constructed it so that you should be able to grasp the main points examined in the programme.

Preliminary reading

Ashton pp. 22–6, 58–62 and 90–5
Hobsbawm pp. 52–62
(*Industrialisation and Culture* C5, D2, F2, F7)

We are going to study the process of innovation, yet in fact we will be concentrating our attention on the cotton industry. Why is this? I want you to begin by asking yourself this question.

More precisely, study the following tables and graphs, then note down what information you derive from each.

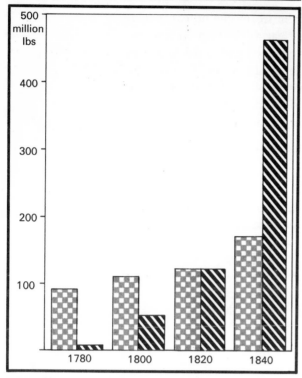

Wool and Cotton Consumption (Britain) 1780-1840

Figure 16

Industry	(a)	(b)	(c)	
			steam	water
Cotton	219	110	46	12
Wool	55	5	17	10
Linen	35	0·3	7	4
Silk	31	2	2	1
Total	340	117·3	72	27

(a)
numbers employed
(1835) in thousands

(b)
power-looms (usually
steam-driven) in
1835, in thousands

(c)
type of power used
in spinning and
weaving (1838) in
thousands of
horsepower

	cost per pound		
	1784	1812	1832
(i) Cotton	10p	7½p	3p
(ii) Wool	4p	8p	6p

SPECIMEN ANSWER

1 Between 1800–20 cotton consumption dramatically catches up, and then overtakes wool.
2 Cotton employs about two-thirds of those employed in the textile industry.
3 It employs practically all the power-looms in the textile industry.
4 It uses steam engines in the proportion 4:1 to water-power whereas 2:1 is the best with other industries.
5 The raw material cost declines far more dramatically in cotton than in wool.

DISCUSSION

1–4 prove quite straightforwardly why we should concentrate on the cotton industry. It was the 'leading sector' of the industrialized production of textiles, significant both in the volume of employment it offered and in the degree of mechanization it achieved. But the reason behind its remarkable expansion is really contained in 5. You will notice that there is a steady decline in the cost of the raw material in cotton which is not reflected in wool.

EXERCISE

Both Ashton (pp. 61–2) and Hobsbawm (pp. 54–6) advance arguments as to why cotton took such a decisive lead over the other textiles.

1 What is Ashton's explanation?
2 What is Hobsbawm's explanation?
3 What similarities do you notice between the two explanations?
4 What differences?
5 Which explanation do you think is most satisfactory and why?

SPECIMEN ANSWER

1   Ashton argues that wool didn't take the lead because of:
(a)   the nature of the material (presumably meaning it was difficult to mechanize)
(b)   ill-advised government regulation
(c)   a market which wasn't expandable.

2   Hobsbawm argues that cotton took the lead because:
(a)   it offered an expanding market and vast profits
(b)   mechanization was cheap
(c)   the supply of raw material could be infinitely expanded
(d)   it did not have to compete with an existing and widespread domestic industry.

3
(a)   Both Ashton (1c) and Hobsbawm (2a) agree that markets for cotton were potentially larger than those for wool.
(b)   They both agree, Ashton (1b) and Hobsbawm (2d), that cotton's newness as an industry was in its favour: it didn't have to overcome vested interests in production and control.
(c)   They both agree Ashton (1a) and Hobsbawm (2b) that mechanization was easier in cotton's case.

4   Where Hobsbawm goes out on his own is in relating the expansion of cotton to the development of slave-worked plantations in the American South (see 2c).

5   My own view would be to favour Hobsbawm, as he takes account of the fall in the cost of raw material as an important factor in increasing production, this being achieved by rapid expansion in cotton cultivation.

DISCUSSION

In my own view, Hobsbawm is right to put his emphasis on the expanding production of raw material. As you can imagine, a raw material that comes straight from a plant, and doesn't have to be digested by a silkworm, grown on the back of a sheep, or treated by repeated steeping in water, like linen flax, is likely to be easier to grow. Production can be expanded simply by bringing more land under cultivation. And labour recruitment problems can be solved simply by importing more slaves.

Here we have seen one of the ways in which Hobsbawm's Marxist analysis has helped broaden the area of debate about the causes and effects of the Industrial

Revolution. In discussing these he extends the geographical area concerned in the changes to include the foreign economies profoundly affected by British industrialization. Later on we'll be dealing with the effect of the Industrial Revolution on the living standards of British working people. But, Hobsbawm would argue, regardless of how we decide this question, we cannot isolate it from the effects on Indian communities of the Manchester cloths which destroyed their native cotton industries, and the effect of the increase in demand for cotton on the strengthening of the slave system of the American South.

Up to now we have been dealing with the general position of cotton in the textile industries, and investigating one reason for its distinctive growth. Now I want to turn to the mechanical processes which made this growth possible.

For a start, read Ashton pp. 22–6 where he deals with the progress of the textile industry in the earlier part of the eighteenth century.

EXERCISE

If you wanted to use the information Ashton gives on pp. 22–6 as a basis for study of the subsequent development, under what *four* major headings would you choose to examine it?

SPECIMEN ANSWER

My four main headings would be:
1 The technical process of manufacture
2 The economic organization of the industry
3 The geographical location of the industry
4 The nature of the produce manufactured

DISCUSSION

The first three were easy to get, the fourth was one of those factors so obvious that we tend to overlook it. Remember that the small amount of cotton imported from Elizabethan times was essentially a 'quality' product, as were, of course, linen and silk goods. Such products were at the mercy of changes in fashion, and these could have a real effect in causing fluctuations in demand. What, however, caused the steady rise in demand for cotton and linen goods after 1750?

Let us put it this way:
1 What sorts of clothes and objects are made from cotton and linen?
2 And what was the position of the demand for such garments at the middle of the eighteenth century?

SPECIMEN ANSWER

1 Shirts, underwear, sheets.
2 If you've been reading your Ashton, you'll see that he attributes a fall in the death-rate to the growing use of cotton underclothes (p. 3).

DISCUSSION

Generally, we can see the growing demand for cotton as part of the social improvements of the early eighteenth century. It's possible also to see the rapid expansion of the use of linen, (more or less interchangeable with cotton) as a result of the migration to Britain of French linen-weaving Protestants after Louis XIV's campaign of repression.

EXERCISE

You have seen the fly-shuttle loom and the spinning jenny demonstrated in our television programme. The fly-shuttle was invented in 1734 but did not come into general use until the 1760s. Can you suggest two reasons for this?

SPECIMEN ANSWER

1 The film showed that an improvement in spinning was necessary to provide enough yarn for the fly-shuttle loom.
2 If the demand for cloth is rising, resistance to innovations which economize on labour will be lessened. Weavers are unlikely to want to adopt a loom which is twice as productive as the normal one, as it means, in a situation of static demand, that only half of them will retain their jobs.

DISCUSSION

This exercise has introduced us to two of the basic concepts we encounter when we study the innovation process in the British textile industry:

1 The situation in which an improvement in one process necessitates an improvement in an associated process.
2 The human and social costs involved in replacing the skill of men with the activity of a machine.

Let's look more closely at (1) first. (If you haven't watched the TV broadcast, have Ashton by you.)

EXERCISE

First, a simple identification test: below you'll find photographs of machines and descriptions of their functions. But they don't match. I want you to allocate the correct description to each machine. Then write, in the space below the photograph, the inventor you associate with each machine.

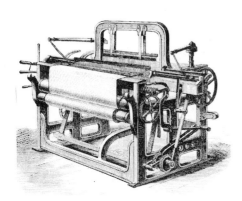

Figure 17

Figure 18

43

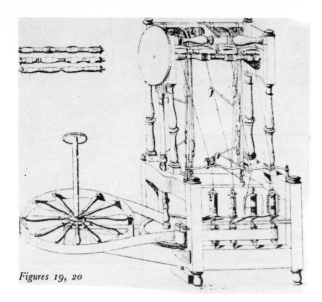

Figures 19, 20

Figures 21, 22

(a) A water-powered machine which draws out 'roved' cotton by three sets of rollers revolving at different speeds, from which it is drawn on to a revolving spindle, and then spun into yarn.

(b) A loom operated by power conveyed to it by an overhead belt from a steam engine.

(c) A machine which brushes the cotton on bristles to prepare it for spinning.

(d) A hand-loom which employs an arrangement of hammers to propel the shuttle to and fro across the warp.

(e) A machine on which, with his left hand, the operator draws out the thread from up to eighty spindles, twisting with his right hand on a single wheel which works the multiple spindles.

(f) A machine which both draws out the roved yarn from its bobbin by rollers and has a carriage of spindles which travels to and fro, stretching and twisting the yarn.

SPECIMEN ANSWER

(I have arranged the machines in the order in which they were invented.)

			invented	adopted
Figure 18	(d)	Kay's flying shuttle.	1734	c1760
Figure 22	(e)	Hargreaves' spinning jenny.	1768	1770
Figure 19	(a)	Arkwright's water frame.	1769	1771
Figure 21	(c)	Arkwright's carding machine.	1775	1775
Figure 20	(f)	Crompton's spinning mule.	1778	1790
Figure 17	(b)	Cartwright's power loom.	1785	c1830

EXERCISE

What reasons do you think manufacturers had for bringing (Figures) 22, 19, 17 into use?

SPECIMEN ANSWER

They wanted more yarn to feed to the improved fly-shuttle looms, hence spinning improvements (Figures 22, 19).

> Once they had exploited these they wanted to mechanize weaving and thus the whole manufacturing process (Figure 17).

DISCUSSION

This raises two points which I want to discuss in greater detail. Why did factory-spinning prove more successful than jenny spinning, which could be carried on in existing domestic workshops? And why did the power loom take so long to come into general use?

These two questions raise an important issue about the introduction of a new technology to an industry. It is highlighted by Ashton (p. 94) when he discusses the reasons for the failure to introduce power-looms more rapidly. Note down a sentence on this page which suggests three reasons why machine-spinning was rapidly adopted while power-loom weaving grew slowly.

SPECIMEN ANSWER

> If there had been in weaving a man of the type of Arkwright, if there had been no immigration and no Poor Law allowance, the transfer to the factory might have been effected quickly and with less suffering.

DISCUSSION

Let's look specifically at Arkwright and his career. Ashton's tribute is well-deserved: if you look at any of the great textile mills which together with his income from his patents, gained him a fortune of half a million pounds in less than twenty years, you see the technical prototype of the mills which constituted the major industrial units of Britain until the 1840s.

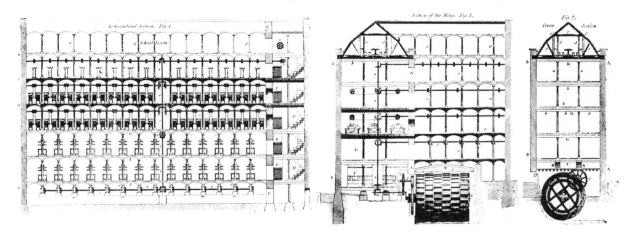

Figure 23

Above is a diagram of the Belper Mill of Arkwright's former partners, the Strutts. You can see the integration of the cotton spinning process – the carding machines, then a series of machines, which, operating like simplified spinning machines, draw out the carded cotton into a loose yarn or 'rove', finally the spinning machines, lower down, all connected by gearing to the water-wheel. If you compare it with a later nineteenth-century mill (Hobsbawm, Figure 75) you will notice little difference in plan apart from the use of steam.

The remarkable thing is that Arkwright set up the factory production of cotton in only four or five years. How did he manage it?

EXERCISE

Right, first try to break this question up. How did Arkwright, a Preston barber in 1768, manage to create Cromford Mill in 1771? (a) Can you think of three main problems he would have to face? Then (b), looking through Ashton pp. 58–9, how did Arkwright deal with each problem?

SPECIMEN ANSWER

(a)
1   How did he invent the water-spinning frame?
2   Where did he come across the factory principle?
3   Where did he raise the money?

(b)
1   He may have taken the idea from Lewis Paul's earlier experiments, and from the work of a contemporary mechanic in Preston, George Highs.
2   In Derbyshire, at the time Arkwright came south from Lancashire, there were several factories spinning (or 'throwing') silk, on which pattern he may have modelled his own plant.
3   He approached the prosperous hosiers of Nottingham for funds.

DISCUSSION

Arkwright can't be credited with much technical ingenuity: most of the inventions he patented were not his own but had been the subject of experiment for several decades. But he grasped the idea that the mechanization of spinning required the creation of a continuous process from receipt of the bale to sale of the spun yarn. In this he was remarkably successful.

Nevertheless, his process to a great extent succeeded despite him. Arkwright demanded a royalty on the installation of all machinery built according to his patent. This could come to £7,000 for every 100 spindles, or, if we take Arkwright's Cromford Mill as a standard, about £35,000 a mill. Which gives one reason for the rapidity of Arkwright's rise to wealth, and shows how profitable cotton-spinning by machine must have been.

Before machine spinning could be totally successful, however, the duties the government charged on manufactured cotton goods had to be reduced. This Arkwright succeeded in doing in 1773. The production of British calicoes rose, as a result of both factors, from 56,814 yards in 1775 to 3,578,590 in 1783.

EXERCISE

Where then did the spinning mule come in?

SPECIMEN ANSWER

The yarn produced by the Arkwright frame was only suitable for weaving coarser cloths, so a finer yarn was required, which the mule supplied.

DISCUSSION

In fact the mule could spin up to a thousand miles of yarn from a pound of cotton, whereas the Arkwright frame's limit was about twenty miles. The mule could not, as you saw in the television programme, be completely automated; a skilled spinner still had to control its movements (although he could spin up to a hundred threads). But it could be adapted to power-drive, and was.

EXERCISE

1   How would the work-force of a mule-spinning factory differ from that of Arkwright's Cromford Mill?
2   Do you think this would have an effect on the siting of a factory?

3 What other innovation of the time do you think might have influenced the siting of textile factories?

4 Why?

SPECIMEN ANSWER

1 It would be a skilled labour force, not one composed of children.

2 There would be a tendency to move to where skilled labour was available, i.e. into the towns.

3 The steam engine, first applied to a textile factory in 1785.

4 Dependence on water-power could now be done away with, which meant that mills need no longer be sited by swift streams in country districts.

DISCUSSION

Mule-spinning and the steam engine created the modern spinning mill. By the 1820s such plants were installed as complete units, with a range of machines based on Arkwright and Crompton prototypes. Mill-design and construction had by this time become an expert activity, carried out by men like William Fairbairn and Richard Roberts (see *Industrialisation and Culture* D2).

Factory Workers and Handloom Weavers in the Cotton Industry 1810-1840

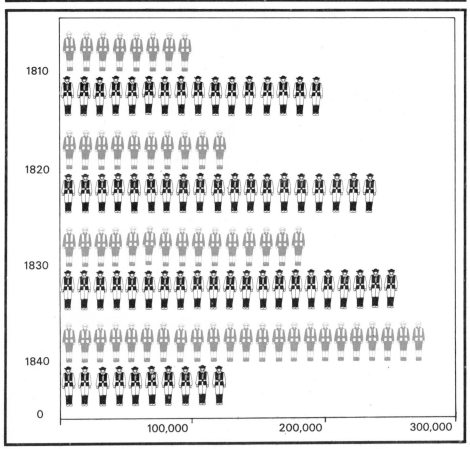

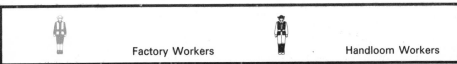

Factory Workers   Handloom Workers

Figure 24

Weaving

But this was only one side of the process. What was happening to weaving? Cartwright's power-loom, as we have seen, was patented in 1785. It was not the first. A power-loom for the weaving of ribbons was in use in England and France in the early seventeenth century; in 1678 another was built by a Frenchman, de Gennes, and later a third by the French engineer Vaucanson. But it took over forty years for the power-loom to come into general use in Britain. Why was this?

Well, here are:

1 a graph of the number of factory workers and the number of hand-loom weavers in the cotton industry, 1806–40 (on previous page)

2 a graph of the amount of the yards of yarn exported as cloth and the spun yarn exported 1820–50;

3 a graph of the earnings of a hand-loom weaving family of six persons, 1814–33.

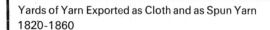

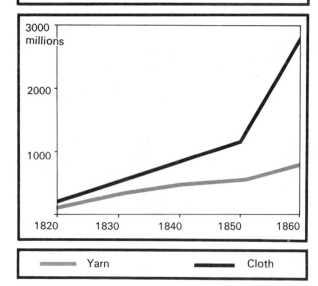

Figure 25

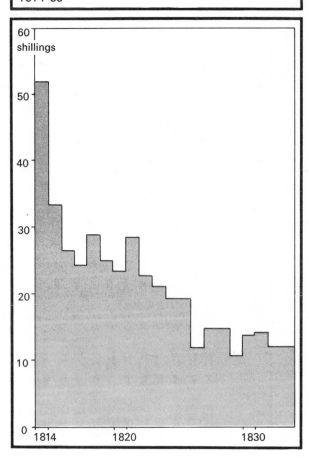

Figure 26

Taking information from the three of these, and adding it to what you know about the history of the power-loom, I want you to use it to evaluate Ashton's and Hobsbawm's explanations of the delay in installing power-looms.

You will find Ashton's account on page 94 and Hobsbawm's on pages 55 and 60. What are the main points of both?

SPECIMEN ANSWER

> Ashton
> Delays were due to:
> 1   imperfection in the power-loom;
> 2   high rates of interest because of the war inhibiting investment;
> 3   dislike of weavers for factory life.

> Hobsbawm
> Keeping weavers many and poor was as much a part of capitalist industrialization as replacing them with machines.

Now, having got the two explanations straight, I want you to go back to the three graphs.

Measuring Ashton and Hobsbawm's accounts against them, who, in your estimation, comes out better and why?

SPECIMEN ANSWER

> I would plump for Hobsbawm for the following reasons:
> 1   Technical difficulties with the loom there may have been, but if the idea could have been successfully demonstrated in the seventeenth century it was surely capable of relatively easy improvement.
> 2   Ashton's argument about the rate of interest deterring investment really won't wash because the number of factory workers still goes up during the rather difficult period 1810–20, indicating substantial investment in plant (Figure 24).
> 3   There seems a quite definite correlation between a growing weaving workforce and declining wages. As wages came down, of course, manufacturers were less willing to invest in expensive power-looms when they could otherwise have their weaving done cheaply by hand (Figure 26).
> 4   Or when they could export yarn instead of weaving it into cloth (Figure 25).

DISCUSSION

My own view, for what it's worth, is that until the power-loom had become significantly cheaper and easier to install, about the late 1820s, the lower cost of hand-weaving delayed the introduction of power-looms. We will go on later to look at the fate of the hand-loom weavers as part of the industrial working class. But first I should like to suggest some factors which may already have occurred to you as possible influences on the course of change in textiles. Both Ashton and Hobsbawm tend to be rather schematic thinkers but, as we've seen earlier, the particular and the local can distort patterns which some hold to be general.

Bear in mind that a wide variety of cotton products could be turned out by hand-loom production. Not all of these could be machine-produced, and some therefore persisted as hand woven fabrics. Fear of reprisals by work people may also have deterred industrialists from installing power-looms but, on the other hand, a new spinning factory in an area remote from weavers might find it profitable to weave by machine from the beginning.

I haven't the space to deal with the development of the other textile industries.

However, there are several observations about them worth making at this stage. First: their technologies were adopted almost without change from the cotton industry, although in the process the machinery acquired a baffling variety of new names, frequently differing from region to region. Secondly, they had not such an intense geographical concentration as the cotton industry. Although the West Riding of Yorkshire was the pre-eminent woollen area, woollen factories were widely dispersed throughout the country and the important tweed industry grew up in an area remote from the coalfields, the Scottish borders, while hand-weavers continued to produce 'homespuns' in Ireland and the Scottish highlands. Finally, the textile industry later employed more women than men. The post-1840 railway-based industrialization tended to be male-employing, so in areas where there were substantial engineering works (for instance Glasgow – see A100 Units 29–30, Section 3.2) textile works tended also to be set up to employ female labour. This contributed to the geographical dispersal of the non-cotton textiles and the clothing industry.

Section 2.6
The Chemical Industry

Preliminary reading
Ashton pp. 62–4
Hobsbawm pp. 327–33, 338–43 (You need not read this in detail.)

Introduction

Ashton's treatment is straightforward enough though, as we shall see, rather limited and not wholly accurate. This is one of those areas of study where even the ablest economic historian shows that he can't always master developments in all of the subjects he studies all of the time.

You may find some of the technical terms Ashton uses baffling at first. So I've provided a list of these and given some notes on them.

reagent	any substance used in a chemical reaction
tinctures	dyes; also 'the essential principle of a substance obtained in a solution'
sulphuric acid	cheapest of the three mineral acids, used to clean iron, and to act on salt to produce hydrochloric acid, oxidized in its turn to chlorine
apothecary	druggist
vitriol	sulphuric acid
chlorine	gas used to bleach and (later) to disinfect
slaked lime	lime heated then crumbled by water, used to counteract over-acid clay soils
soda	alkaline substance used in the manufacture of glass and soap
white lead	pigment, containing lead, used in paint
litharge	an oxide of lead used in pottery as glaze; 'red lead', a separate oxide, is used in paint
potash	corrosive alkali substance taken from ashes of burnt plants, used in the manufacture of potassium nitrate for fertilizers, and soap making
alum	combination of potassium and aluminium sulphate used in paper making, leather making, dyeing
ammonia	colourless pungent gas, soluble in water, used for manufacture of fertilizer and smelling salts
Leblanc process	soda was produced by heating common salt with sulphuric acid and heating the product with limestone and coal
Berthollet process	a method of bleaching by chlorine
sal ammoniac	ammonium chloride, corrosive solid used in dyeing cloth

EXERCISE

As you can see from Ashton's account, chemical progress seems to have had two main industrial implications.

1 In what main fields of industry were these?
2 What difference in the relationship of industry to invention do you see between the two?

SPECIMEN ANSWER

> 1 These were (a) dyes and bleaches for textiles: and (b) products associated with the exploitation of coal.

> 2 In the case of the textile industries, chemical progress seems to have come about through industrial demand, while in coal it arose as a by-product of the main industry.

DISCUSSION

This is a very simplified picture but one which, I think, sets the chemical industry in its general economic context. At one level it was a very wide-ranging business altogether, as no human activity excludes the use of some chemical or other. However the chemicals used were primitive or traditional, or where new processes were used they were only marginal in their effect. Pottery and paper making are cases in point: both industries expanded, in both improved processes were introduced during our period, but the main motors of change were mechanical or organizational and the aggregate size of the industry did not change to an extent which demanded a complete chemical revolution.

In textiles this revolution had to come, or the slowness of traditional techniques of bleaching and dyeing would in its turn have slowed up the machine production of fabric. Bleachfields and print-works, although their names suggest a certain casualness of organization, were by the early nineteenth century as mechanized as the factories which supplied them. As Ashton indicates, the underlying theoretical knowledge was French, and significantly, reached Britain through the only practicable channels – medical men and the Scottish Universities which, alone of the British universities, gave an education which was scientific in orientation. But the application of these techniques depended on demand and capital on the scale which the industrialization of textiles generated.

On the other hand, the chemical industries using coal developed as by-products of the central business of producing coke for iron smelting. Coke is produced by heating coal in the absence of air in a 'retort'. As well as coke, which burns at a higher temperature than coal, this process gives off inflammable gases and tars. By the 1780s coal tar was being produced, as an alternative to wood-based tar and pitch, and in the early 1800s coal gas was being used for mill and house lighting: in both cases war may have been influential in hastening development, as supplies both of 'naval stores' – pitch and tar – and whale-oil were threatened by the enemy.

It is difficult to generalize about the role of research in the 'scientific' innovations of the period, – but it seems plausible to argue that the practical mechanic rather than the academic researcher took the limelight: although the level of scientific discussion in the circle around Boulton and Watt at Birmingham was high, including Joseph Priestley, James Keir the chemist, and Erasmus Darwin, Watt's skilled engine-fitter William Murdock was as noteworthy for his construction of the first practicable gas-making retorts. While the great Humphry Davy's name is connected with the miner's safety lamp, George Stephenson, an illiterate, and William Clanny, a doctor, produced quite independently a very similar lamp. Laboratory-based research had yet to make a substantial impact on industry; when it did, from the late 1820s in Germany and France, it passed Britain by.

Section 2.7
The Manufacture of Household Goods

Preliminary reading
Ashton pp. 64–6

EXERCISE

First of all I want you to go back to the working-class interior we looked at in the section on the iron industry. I want you to make a list of the non-metal items of the room, and, try to decide whether, in the light of what they're made of, you would regard the way these were produced in 1830 as a *handcraft* or a *factory-based industry*.

SPECIMEN ANSWER

window-glass	factory-based industry
carpets	factory-based industry
furniture	handcraft
curtains	factory-based industry
newspapers	factory-based industry
books	factory-based industry
pottery	factory-based industry
barrels	handcraft
glassware	factory-based industry

DISCUSSION

By and large we can take it that carpets and curtains were subject to the same sort of changes in production that affected the textile industry (Section 2.5). Furniture, substantially a handcraft-based industry (although the tools used in such handcrafts improved dramatically over our period) and coopering, the making of barrels, in which were stored all sorts of foodstuffs as well as wine and beer, were, and remained until very recently, highly-skilled handcraft industries.

So let's take each of the rest – pottery, window-glass and glassware, paper and printing – in turn.

Pottery

EXERCISE

Ashton's account we can take to be a reasonably effective and accurate one. I intend here to expand on certain aspects of it. But before I do I'd like you to try to note down what Ashton considers to be the main changes.

52

SPECIMEN ANSWER

1	Expansion of demand	Not enough lead and tin, more tea and coffee drinking
2	Use of new techniques and materials	e.g. China clay, 'Queen's Ware'
3	Intensification of division of labour	
4	Use of transport to co-ordinate supplies	e.g. The Grand Junction Canal

DISCUSSION

Now we've already discussed one aspect of the effect of growing domestic demand on industrial expansion in Section 2.5, so I don't intend to deal further with it here.

As to the *division of labour*, those of you who have come through A100 Units 29–30 should be reasonably familiar with this concept. If you've not, here's a contemporary picture of some of the processes into which the production of pottery was subdivided at Etruria works.

Making of the clay, dishes, plates, &c. upon moulds or casts of various forms and patterns.

A Potters Oven when firing or baking, the ware being therein placed in Safeguards, or "Saggers."

EXERCISE

Now I don't want you to look in detail at each of these processes, but simply to answer the question: why did the division of labour reduce the cost of the product? If you have it to hand, you can best do this by looking at the extract from Adam Smith's *Wealth of Nations* in *Industrialisation and Culture* H1. What is his main justification for the division of labour?

SPECIMEN ANSWER

That by a number of men concentrating on specialized jobs a high rate of productivity was achieved, each man making 4,800 pins instead of 20.

DISCUSSION

Such improved productivity could not by itself have given pottery its important position as a part of domestic life. The quality of the product also increased.

Pottery, as we know from archaeological excavations, has been a part of domestic life from prehistoric times. However, its range of uses was limited while it remained crude in execution, rough in surface, and heavy. The poor, while using pottery jars and bottles, preferred wood for plates and bowls, and horn for cups; the wealthy used pewter or silver.

By the seventeenth century imported china became popular in wealthier households of Europe and in that century the first factories began to be set up. Delft in Holland was the first major European centre, followed by works at Meissen in Saxony (1710) and Sèvres in France (1738) which were founded under Royal patronage. The first British works were founded in imitation of the great continental concerns.

However, the clientele of such works was essentially aristocratic. Although they set a fashion, their production could not be expanded. The achievement of Wedgwood and his Staffordshire colleagues was that by setting out to make pottery of roughly the appearance of the quality continental product available to the middling wealth of English towns, farm-house and rectories, they succeeded in doing much more: in creating a new market for pottery among all ranks of society.

I would like to leave you to consider one thing: could Wedgwood have succeeded to the same extent in France?

Window-glass and glassware

Ashton doesn't deal at all with changes in the manufacture of glass, yet these were important. In the mid-eighteenth century glass was a rarity in the windows of the houses of the rural poor: by 1830 it was in general use: and a great era of the use of glass as a major construction material, culminating in the great railway terminals and the Crystal Palace, was just about to begin. Why was this? Basically because improvements in glass-making had led to an expansion and cheapening of production.

Prior to 1800 window-glass was 'Crown glass'. Thereafter more and more use was made of 'cast glass'. Before I explain the two methods you will want to know how glass – pure and simple – is made: basically by smelting special silica sand with alkaline salts in a crucible-furnace.

'Crown glass' was blown – you are probably familiar enough with the process of glass-blowing. However, once the globe of blown glass was formed it was transferred to a metal rod, which the glass maker revolved rapidly so that the globe, still kept hot and fluid, expanded outwards by centrifugal force until it became a disk out of which panes could be cut. It still had a lump of thicker glass in the centre, forming the 'whorls' you'll see in older houses' windows.

'Cast glass' was, on the other hand, prepared rather like cast iron.

The molten glass was poured from the crucible (a) on to a leather-covered table; and spread out by the roller (b).

It was then polished by grinding on a flat stone surface by a horizontal grindstone and subsequently buffed to smoothness.

Figure 28

Now this process was devised in France, and a large monopolistic factory set up, in 1688. And emigré French workmen helped set up the first British factory in 1776, at St. Helens in Lancashire. Because of the effect of soot on molten glass the use of charcoal continued until 1792, when covered pots for melting glass were introduced at St. Helens. Thereafter a move to the coalfields took place and some of the factories constructed in the St. Helens and Newcastle area were among the largest industrial structures in Britain.

Paper making and printing

At its most primitive, paper was made by chewing up old rags in water, then dipping a sieve-like tray into the mixture, squeezing the resulting layer and drying it.

Towards the end of the eighteenth century this process was improved by making it continuous and mechanically operated.

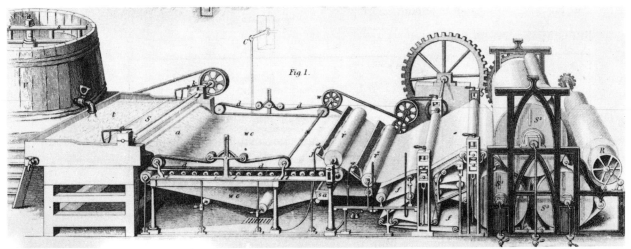

Figure 29

EXERCISE

Here is a picture of a paper-making machine of about 1820. How do you think it operated?

SPECIMEN ANSWER

> It picked up the pulp by a continuous belt-sieve, then passed the layer of
> pulp through rollers to squeeze it.

DISCUSSION

The paper was subsequently passed through heated rollers to dry it, then
bleached by the use of the same chemicals which were applied to cloth. Many
water and steam-operated mills were set up in Lancashire and Midlothian in
Scotland. Wallpaper was produced in the same way as printed cloth, by running
it through a cylinder-press and, after 1814, the steam engine was applied to
print *The Times*: a cylinder pressed sheets of paper on to a flat type-bed. Half
a century however passed before the modern principle of 'rotary cylinder-
printing' was applied to newspaper printing, because of the complicated pre-
paration of the type-cylinders, a prohibitively time-consuming process before
the development of sophisticated typesetting machinery.

Another element in the modern paper and print industry missing until the
mid-nineteenth century was the use of woodpulp shipped from Canada. This
provided a cheap raw material for the mass-circulation newspaper press of
the end of the century, but was essentially the product of the later industrialization of transport.

Section 2.8
Transport Changes

Preliminary reading
Ashton pp. 34–8, 66–71
Hobsbawm pp. 49, 63–5
(*Industrialisation and Culture* E1, E2)

EXERCISE

First of all, try to estimate the requirements of industry for improved transport.
One way to do this is to go through the industries we've studied so far, and
estimate the requirements of each.

SPECIMEN ANSWER

> Agriculture
> required transport to bring fertilizer to the land and to carry away arable
> crops (cattle and sheep were still driven on the hoof).
> Coal industry
> used sea transport to convey coal to London from the North East. Primitive
> railways used to connect mines with water transport.
> Iron industry
> used sea transport to import iron ore; water or road transport to bring
> lime works usually on a coalfield by end of century.
> The steam engine
> until 1800 most of these were built in the West Midlands, which meant
> that engineers had to travel out from Birmingham by road to install them.
> The textile industry
> used sea transport to import cotton; road transport at first to water mills
> in valleys, then canals. Then had to transport coal to work steam engines.

Chemicals

centred mainly on deposits of salt, from which the country was supplied. Coal had to be taken by road or canal to gas-works.

Household goods

again geographical concentration – glass at St. Helens, pottery in North Staffordshire, paper in Lancashire and Midlothian – transported throughout the country.

DISCUSSION

The Industrial Revolution implied a high degree of *regional specialization*. Of course, there had been specialized production before, but this had usually been tied to a *large local market*. Difficulties of transport meant that the range of goods produced was not wide, and that their price was high.

Basically, every town tended to have a range of skills and techniques available which could fabricate from imported raw material the limited number of consumer goods demanded by the locality. Certain topographical factors affected even this primitive situation, however. The woollen industry was largely confined to areas with soft water, the iron industry had to be sited in woodlands where charcoal could be made, salt-works which used brine were necessarily by the seashore.

In the eighteenth century the supply of fuel came greatly to determine the siting of industry.

Industry moved to where the bulkiest raw material was. For instance, in the iron industry about 1800 (subject to wide regional variations) a ton of iron required up to eight tons of coal, one ton of limestone and only three tons of iron ore. So the general tendency was to situate the ironworks on a coalfield, on the grounds that it was cheaper to transport a ton of iron to a relatively distant market than to transport eight tons of coal to an ironworks near that market.

EXERCISE

Here is a map (Figure 30) dated about 1800 of the situation of the famous Carron Ironworks, which was founded in 1759 in Scotland to smelt iron with coke. What sorts of transport do the works use, and for what purposes?

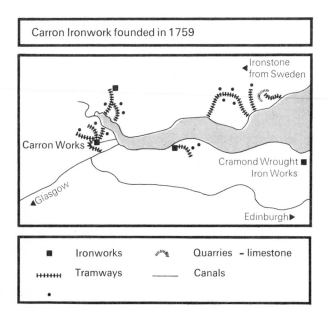

Figure 30

SPECIMEN ANSWER

(a) Iron ore came by ship from Sweden, up the short canal to the works.
(b) Coal was mined locally and brought to the works by tramroad.
(c) Limestone was quarried in Fife and brought to the works by tramroad and ship.
(d) Manufactured iron was transported away from the works by canal to Glasgow or shipped coastwise.

DISCUSSION

For most of our period the work of railways was generally similar to that of the lines at Carron: feeding another form of transportation. There were several hundred miles of such lines in operation by 1830, mainly in Northumberland and South Wales, some of which were worked by primitive steam locomotives (adapted from Richard Trevithick's high-pressure engine of 1800). But the main components of the national transport system remained the coasting ships, the canal, the navigable river, and the turnpike road.

Turnpikes

'Turnpike' simply means 'toll'. In other words the 'improved' road was paid for by its users paying charges at toll-gates. This money enabled interest to be paid on funds raised to carry out improvements, like widening, straightening, resurfacing, and replacing fords with bridges. Such improvements meant that *wheeled* traffic could now use the roads. Under the old system of 'statute labour' – compulsory work by locals – roads were badly maintained and generally unsuitable for wheeled traffic.

Before road improvements became a major concern, official policy was in fact to *deter* traffic, or to regulate it in such a way that it caused as little damage to road surfaces as possible.

This was done by measures such as regulating the size of vehicles' wheels. The narrower the tread of a wheel, the deeper the rut it left in the road, and the greater amount of damage it did to the road. Quarter-sessions and parish officials often required vehicles to have broad treads, which harmed the road less, but were unpopular with carriers because they made vehicles heavier and slower.

What this amounted to was an attempt to cut the traffic to suit the road rather than an attempt to produce roads which could cope with an increased traffic. But after the improvements in road-making technology, and the widespread adoption of turnpike trusts, such measures were dropped in favour of a policy of general improvement.

Generally, we tend to think of turnpikes as major roads, but in fact they embraced most of the roads which are 'A' and 'B' roads today. County authorities would secure 'general' turnpiking acts and institute a county-wide system.

Along with turnpiking on the roads (see Figure 31) came a remarkable increase in travel speeds. This was partly the result of a better surface and easier gradients, and partly the result of the better organization of coach services. The government took a leading part in this by subsidizing, through mail contracts, the long-distance coaches. What had been a slow and unexacting journey was

Figure 31

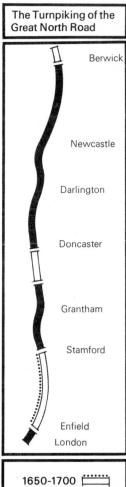

The Turnpiking of the Great North Road

Berwick

Newcastle

Darlington

Doncaster

Grantham

Stamford

Enfield
London

1650-1700
1700-1750
1750-1800

58

replaced by a fast timetabled run, in which teams of horses were driven as fast as possible between stages, and then changed. In this way journey times were drastically reduced. London to Glasgow took two weeks in 1750, two days in 1830 (see Hobsbawm Figure 81).

Navigable rivers and canals

At the end of the unit is a map of British waterways in 1830.

The map shows:

(a) the dimensions of the barges which could be accommodated by canals and navigable rivers;

(b) the dates at which navigations were opened.

EXERCISE

1 What sort of navigations were opened up to 1760?

2 What do you think their main disadvantages were?

3 What function did the navigations opened between 1760 and 1770 perform?

4 What do you notice about the pattern of navigation promotion, 1760–1800? Is it even or does it rise into peaks? If so, when?

5 In Ashton's view, what motive would have driven cash into canal promotion in 1792?

6 What difficulties do you think underlay the operation of the British canals as a system of transport in 1830?

SPECIMEN ANSWER

1 Navigable rivers.

2 The inability to navigate from river network to river network, save by sea. In other words, it was impossible to take a barge from London to Leeds.

3 They linked together the river networks of the Trent, the Mersey, and the Severn; thus making the inland waterways of Britain into a system.

4 There are two big peaks of construction, between 1760 and 1770, and between 1790 and 1795.

5 Money went into canals because it wasn't in demand from the government, because of peace and good harvests.

6 Difficulties were caused by different dimensions of locks throughout the country, meaning that, for example, a boat 60′ × 12′ couldn't sail from London further than Birmingham, nor could it use the broad canals of the North.

DISCUSSION

First let's deal with the difference between a navigable river and a canal. There are really two: one is legal – a river is a natural phenomenon, which has for generations been subject to legal claims for purposes other than navigation – water supply, boundaries, fords, fishing, etc., the second is physical – you don't have to supply water to a river.

Now Ashton makes a distinction between the development of river navigations and the engineer-made canals (p. 38). I think this has to be challenged: river navigations remained important transport arteries – the Thames, Severn, Trent and Yorkshire Ouse – and their importance was enhanced rather than diminished by the canals. The 1760 period was not as decisive, technically, as Ashton makes out: in an essay presented to him on his retirement T. C. Barker (Barker, 1960) proved that the skills of canal-building (the techniques of supplying and retaining water) were known about forty years before Brindley's Bridgwater canal: the first proper canal in the British Isles was in fact in Ireland, between Lough Neagh and Newry, and was sponsored by the government as early as 1730. And what Ashton calls (p. 38) 'the canalization of the little Sankey Brook' was in fact the construction of a proper canal in Lancashire not a dozen miles from the site of the future Bridgwater canal. Moreover, the techniques used to build mill-races and dams for water-wheels could also easily be applied to canal construction.

So we can say that there was no great increase in civil engineering skills at the mid-century, but rather that demand existed for inland navigation, and the cash existed to provide it: together these sponsored increased opportunities for civil engineers and, ultimately, an expanded and sophisticated profession.

The trouble was that canals were still built to varying standards, and this made their operation as a system difficult. In fact, technically they stagnated until the twentieth century, with their gaily-painted 'narrow boats' hauled by horse and carrying the boatman and his family in their tiny cabins. (When we go on to consider the question of the standard of life you might find it interesting to keep this group in mind – in many ways their life was hard in the extreme, but their independence and unique culture made them a distinctive and proud race.)

What were the reasons for this stagnation? It's worth while looking closely at this phenomenon – technical stagnation in an advanced economy – because it has dogged the British economy ever since; I think the canals were the first important example of it. Why was steam not used on the canals? Largely because they were 'narrow' (see Figure 32), operated effectively enough with horses, and it was felt, with reason, that steam tugs would simply wash away the banks. On the other hand, it was technically quite feasible to rebuild the canal network to a larger capability. Why was this not done? The last important 'broad' canal, the Grand Junction, was opened in 1812, and eighteen years were to pass before the opening of the Liverpool and Manchester railway brought an effective rival on the scene.

There was, obviously enough, an unsettled economic situation: and there was some rivalry from railway schemes, few of which were actually built, but the construction of branch canals, as you can see from the map, went on. My argument is this: the proprietors of canals were doing reasonably, in some cases very, well. A £100 share in the Oxford Canal bought in 1790 was in 1833 worth £595. If, to broaden the canal to take, say, twenty per cent more traffic, it's necessary to halve the dividend, this will gain little favour with shareholders – that is, until such time as a rival appears, and then shareholders may prefer to ditch the canal and buy the rival's shares. Which is what, by and large, they did. The result was that, in face of railway competition, the canals remained archaic, closed or were taken over, and thus a valuable transport asset was allowed to decay.

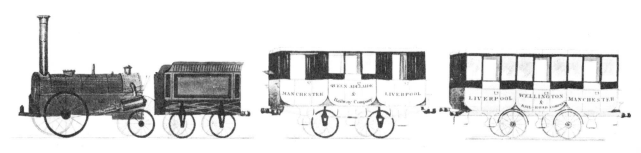

Railways

Figure 34

At the end of the unit is a map of railways in Britain in 1838

EXERCISE

1   Which lines would you identify as:
(a)   horse-worked mineral lines built 1600–1800;
(b)   horse-worked lines constructed as public railways;
(c)   early steam-operated railways;
(d)   the second generation of steam-operated lines, connecting major towns?
2   When do you think we can begin to talk of a railway network?
3   What do you see as a major obstacle to the functioning of this network?
4   Does this obstacle have any parallel in canal history?

SPECIMEN ANSWER

> 1 (a)   Lines on the coalfields: in North-East England and South Wales.
> (b)   Lines like the Surrey Iron Railway, or the Stratford and Moreton Railway.
> (c)   The Stockton and Darlington Railway; the Liverpool and Manchester Railway.
> (d)   The Grand Junction Railway; the London and Birmingham Railway; the Great Western Railway.
> 2   Not until the last of these lines was being built, in 1838.
> 3   The lines were being built to a variety of gauges, so through running would be difficult.
> 4   This is similar to the problems caused by the variety of canal lock dimensions.

DISCUSSION

The railway didn't emerge as an alternative transport system until right at the end of our period (see A100 Units 29–30). I won't try to duplicate my earlier treatment, but I'll ask you to try to identify the main points for yourself.

EXERCISE

Above is a drawing of a train of the Liverpool and Manchester Railway of 1830, the first really successful steam-worked railway.
1   What items in the train would you consider traditional in design?
2   What items owe their origin to the inventions of the Industrial Revolution?
3   What major problems do you think had to be overcome before the 'new' elements (2) could be successfully combined with the traditional ones?

SPECIMEN ANSWER

> 1   The wagons and coaches.
> 2   The locomotive is a development of the steam engine of Watt, the wheels and rails were produced by the improvements in the iron industry.

3   The steam engine had to be adapted to run on rails; and the rails themselves had to be sufficiently reliable to permit trains to function at speed.

DISCUSSION

The railway was a fusion of two technologies radically improved by the Industrial Revolution: mechanical engineering and iron making. The commercial structure which produced the canals existed already to finance it, but the process of technical adaptation was a lengthy one: a steam locomotive capable of dealing with fast passenger as well as freight traffic was not perfected until 1829.

Once this break through had been made, the new technology rapidly crystallized, and then, as capital flowed into it, expanded with shattering rapidity. From practically zero in 1830, the railway mileage of Britain rose to 8,000 by 1850, in which £240,000,000 was invested.

EXERCISE

Read through Hobsbawm pp. 63–5.
1   Does Hobsbawm believe the railway expansion was *fundamentally* the development of an essential advance in transportation? If not, what was it?
2   Hobsbawm credits the railway with being 'the basic invention which was to transform the capital goods industries'. What does he mean by this, and what is its significance?
3   Where, according to Hobsbawm, did the capital for railways come from?

SPECIMEN ANSWER

1   No, the railway was really important as an industry which *used* surplus capital and in so doing changed the structure of industry away from textiles and towards capital goods.
2   By 'transforming the capital goods industries' Hobsbawm means that the railway expanded the industries which produced the equipment and materials for further industrialization – like iron, coal and engineering.
3   The money for investment came from the surpluses accruing to the middle and upper classes through their exploitation of the labouring classes.

DISCUSSION

Hobsbawm sees the expansion of the railway as a classic example of the effect of the accumulation of capital acquired by the capitalists by exploiting the 'surplus value' of the labour they employed. The theory of 'surplus value' formulated by Marx was that the labourer was only paid what would keep him alive and working, call this sum 100, while the manufacturer sold the product of his workman's labour at, say, 180, and pocketed the difference. According to Marx, and later to Hobsbawm, the accumulation of such profits from cotton and land flowed in torrents into railway schemes which were not in themselves profitable.

Now, this is an impressive and, to me, up to a point a convincing theory. But we must ask certain questions of it: for a start, to say that capital accumulates is not to say that it builds railways and so restructures the economy. Capital could and, to some extent, did, go in other directions – abroad, into other industries, or into 'conspicuous consumption': mansions and yachts. Why then did it go into railways? Hobsbawm hits near the mark with his evocation of the railway as the drama of the new age. But there was more to this than mere romanticism: the railway was a violent threat to existing communities: it shaped the consciousness of the people who mattered. Not to have a railway station was, for a town, a sign of decline. The railway revolution wasn't critical in the carriage of goods, or even in mass passenger transport until the 1870s, but it changed the pace at which the propertied community lived, where it lived, and what places mattered to it. It was really the pre-eminent symbol of industrialism – it could not have existed without the Industrial Revolution, and it made it manifest throughout the country.

Section 2.9
Business organization

Preliminary reading
Ashton pp. 76–81

EXERCISE

All of you will have some dealings with contemporary firms, working for them, negotiating with them, owning shares in them, and so on. And you should therefore have some idea about how they are organized.

1 How, in the most general terms, do most present-day firms raise their money, and how are they controlled?
2 What forms of raising finance are discussed by Ashton?
3 How do the concerns mentioned by Ashton differ from the modern pattern?
4 Going back to the financial organization of the modern firm, what form of enterprise of the Industrial Revolution period (which we have discussed) does it bear a fairly close resemblance to?

SPECIMEN ANSWER

1 Present-day firms, by and large, tend to raise money by the selling of shares to *shareholders*, who then delegate the overall control of the firm to a *board of directors* who appoint a professional management.
2 Ashton's picture of the firms of the Industrial Revolution is of concerns formed by family units re-investing their profits, or small groups of partners raising, where necessary, additional funds for capital equipment – that is, buildings and machinery – by mortgaging it, and getting on credit the funds necessary to purchase raw materials and pay labour.
3 The difference is the absence of a large number of 'sleeping partner' shareholders.
4 The closest resemblance to the modern company is in the financing of canals and railways by 'joint-stock' companies, which had a mass of inactive shareholders and a board of directors.

DISCUSSION

Ashton's treatment is straightforward and in itself raises few problems, as long as you know what a mortgage is. However, since Ashton wrote, a great amount of research has been carried on into the firms of the Industrial Revolution which has tended to change our picture of their finances. Ashton's stress on the machinery for raising fixed capital has been challenged, in the case of several of the most important industries, by research which puts stress on the guaranteeing of working capital. For instance, here is a list of the 'fixed' and 'working' capital of several concerns compiled by Professor Sidney Pollard.[1]

1 Pollard, S. (1964) 'Fixed Capital in the Industrial Revolution in Britain', *Journal of Economic History*, vol. XXIV, p. 301.

	Fixed Capital	Value of stock of material on hand
Ambrose Crowley's Ironworks (1728)	£12,000	£93,000
Bersham Iron Furnace (1735)	£170	£1,245
Llangavelach (Swansea) Copper Works (1745)	£5,400	£37,700
Stockport Silk Mill (1762)	£2,800	£13,900

EXERCISE

In these circumstances, where the fixed capital can be as little as ten per cent of the working capital, what must the main concern of the partners in the venture be?

SPECIMEN ANSWER

> Obviously to safeguard their credit – by ensuring that they can always guarantee a market for their goods, and thus get their raw materials and labour costs 'on tick'.

DISCUSSION

According to Professor Pollard – and his argument seems to me a compelling one – the critical problem was that of finding working or 'circulating' capital. This, he argues, was achieved simply by expanding credit arrangements familiar enough to merchants and to manufacturers who operated the 'putting-out' system (Ashton pp. 23–5). The difference was that the entrepreneur had previously very low fixed capital costs – warehouses and possibly some simple equipment for handworkers, if they didn't own it themselves. Now his fixed capital proportion, if he had a centralized works or factory, was greater. This meant that the risk he and his partners ran was greater.

EXERCISE

Think of circumstances which might bring, say, a cotton manufacturer to grief.

SPECIMEN ANSWER

> What happened if the market dried up, say because of a war? Then the merchant who guaranteed the manufacturer's market couldn't sell his products, so his suppliers of raw material withheld credit, and he went bust.

DISCUSSION

But, on the other hand, the extra capital invested in buildings and machinery enabled him to produce more cheaply. So, the chances were that if he avoided this sort of crisis, he would do very well. We must also remember that the State laid a limit on the rate which could be paid out as interest on a loan. This remained at five per cent until the 1820s. So there could be no automatic demand by creditors for a proportionate share of the profits when they started to escalate (as modern shareholders would insist today). Which partly accounts for the staggering personal fortunes made by pioneers of the cotton industry like Richard Arkwright, David Dale and Robert Owen. They succeeded almost by sleight of hand, by cleaning up before their creditors and customers realized just how profitable the new industry was.

As their attitude to these 'usury laws' shows, entrepreneurs were quite willing to play along with State control of aspects of the economy where it suited them. Similarly, and Ashton admits it (pp. 102–6), they were not doctrinaire individualists when a bit of price-fixing suited them better. This arose, to a great extent, out of the need to protect their credit. Cut-throat competition could damage the assured market which was necessary to enable firms to raise credit for working capital, and jeopardize an entire industry.

Section 2.10
Banking

Preliminary reading
Ashton pp. 81–7

The main purpose of this section is to simplify a compact but rather complicated treatment of how British banking worked.

One of the first problems you'll encounter is the technical terms Ashton uses. So I've provided explanations of these.

p. 81	providing accommodation for the State	loaning cash to the State
	joint-stock note issue	(see Section 2.10, p. 68)
	merchant bank	means what it says
	bullion	gold, silver
	foreign exchange	cash involved in dealings with abroad
	bills of exchange drawn by traders	see Ashton top of p. 82
p. 82	commission	} should be familiar enough to you as a consumer
	discount	
	mercer	dealer in fabrics and cloth
p. 83	remittances	the settling of accounts for materials etc.
	London correspondent bank	bank which dealt with relations with central banking system
	promissory notes	look closely at your pound note
p. 84	mortgage	this should be familiar enough to you
	shortage of liquid resources	shortage of usable cash
p. 85	mobilizing of short term funds	mobilizing of cash to cover credits for short period
p. 86	brokers	men who bought and sold
	the Funds and East India stock	(see Section 1.2, p. 12)
	public utility	canals, waterworks, gas companies
	bill-brokers	dealers in bills of exchange
	annuities and stock	you should be familiar enough with these
	friendly societies	working-class institutions for insurance
	factories	trading stations in India (and Canada)
p. 87	British National Debt	(see Section 1.2, p. 12)
	French rentes	French investments
	impersonal capital	capital not subject to the particular occupational concern of an individual

As you can see, none of these categories are particularly complicated, and we come across many of them in our own lives as consumers and householders. What we must do now is to see how banking functioned in practice.

EXERCISE

Imagine yourself the owner of a cotton factory. You have paid off the 'capital costs' of your factory – the buildings and machinery – in full, but you will still have two major outgoings – wages and paying for raw materials – and one source of income – the sale of the finished product.

1   In what form would you
    (a)   pay for your raw materials;
    (b)   pay wages?

SPECIMEN ANSWER

> (a)   You would get these on credit, on the security of your being able to sell the finished product.

> (b)   You would have to pay cash, but you might use tokens or a 'truck' system.

EXERCISE

2   How did your transaction in getting the raw material on credit influence the monetary system?

SPECIMEN ANSWER

> The merchant from whom you bought the goods made out a *bill of exchange* which he could then use as a banknote to the value of the sum you owed him.

EXERCISE

3   Assuming the merchant wanted cash, whom would he approach:
   (a)   you
   (b)   a 'country banker'
   (c)   the Bank of England
and what would the one of these he had chosen do? (Underline your choice and explain why.)

SPECIMEN ANSWER

> (a)   He wouldn't approach you before the term of your credit was up, as you wouldn't have sold enough cloth to pay him.

> (b)   He would approach a *country banker* who would pay him cash (less a charge) or, in other words, 'discount' your bill. He then became your creditor.

> (c)   He wouldn't approach the Bank of England as his name (and yours), wouldn't be important enough to persuade the Bank to exchange cash for a bill.

EXERCISE

4   Let us assume, however, that the country banker is pressed for cash. He can't approach you: what then must he do?
5   What are the two dangers that face him?

SPECIMEN ANSWER

> 4   He sends your bill to his 'corresponding bank' in London who sends him cash if it can exchange his bill for it with the Bank of England.

> 5 (a)   That you won't be able to sell your goods and meet your debt.
> (b)   That a government demand for coin might make the Bank of England refuse to pay cash, in which case he's in trouble if there is a demand for cash in his locality.

EXERCISE

6   What circumstances might bring about such dangers?

7   Think of two of Ashton's general conclusions, which we have already discussed, that might be reinforced by this study of banking.

SPECIMEN ANSWER

> 6 War both threatened the manufacturers' markets, and, by increasing the government's demand for cash, diverted funds from discounting bills to the government.

> 7 Ashton concentrates particularly on the *destructive effect of war* and on the *disadvantages of government intervention* in the economy.

DISCUSSION

In the last analysis, then, the Bank of England would 'cover' a whole succession of 'paper transactions' be lending its own gold coin in return for endorsed bills: but it would only do this if (a) the bill was worth its face value (in other words that it would be honoured at the other end) and if (b) its gold were not required elsewhere, especially by the government or by foreign creditors.

EXERCISE

Imagine a very bad harvest in Britain: what sequence of events will ensue, and what repercussions will these have on the banking system?

SPECIMEN ANSWER

> A bad harvest means imports of grain; imports have to be paid for in gold so there is an outflow of gold from the country; the Bank of England will therefore be less willing to discount bills. At some stage in the banking system, therefore, there will be a demand for cash which can't be met, and the country banker will tend to be caught in this position and forced to the wall.

DISCUSSION

For the businessman the situation was made worse because to attract gold back into the country, the government would lower the price of its own stocks, causing the *effective* rate of interest to rise (say, £100 stock at four per cent might drop to £90), and making investors buy them instead of putting their money in commerce and industry.

Thus industry was subjected to a pincer-like squeeze by events like foreign wars or bad harvests, and the relationships of credit and cash were so constructed that the effects of such upsets were multiplied. We'll deal in Part 3 with the commerical depressions which punctuated the post-1815 years, but at this stage we had better take note of the role the supply of cash could play in causing them.

Now you'll have noticed that one claw of this 'pincer grip' didn't appear to have much to do with industrial activity: this was the Bank of England's desire to preserve its gold for foreign exchange. This affected merchants trading abroad, but not manufacturers. They tended to see it as a humbug: an unnecessary restriction on their own expansion. So they tended to favour a supply of money which was tied to *the levels of production* in the country, and not to the Bank of England's stock of gold.

67

To the banking world, and the semi-professional economists who were close to it, like David Ricardo, such views were heretical as they would lead to an unstable and inflationary currency. Money (in the shape of notes) was put into circulation which could not directly be exchanged for gold, consequently could fall in value and contribute to a disastrous inflation.

Heresy was not confined to the manufacturers – who put it into practice by circulating their own coin and notes (Figure 35) (John Wilkinson was a notable example). Country bankers, ground between their clients' demands for cash and the Bank of England's unwillingness to lend, wanted a more flexible money system too. This could, and sometimes did, drive them to a radical political stance. Thomas Attwood, the leader of the Birmingham radicals in the 1820s and 1830s, was a banking and currency reformer as well. But the reformers never succeeded in weakening the grip of the Bank of England: although during the war period 1797–1821 the exchange of gold for notes was suspended, payments in gold were resumed after the emergency was over and orthodoxy was maintained.

At this stage it's fair to ask just what effect this tension between central and local banking did in fact have on commercial expansion. Ashton makes the point that, with strong joint-stock banks, there was more stability for commerce in Scotland. While this is true, there seems to be no significant difference between English and Scottish rates of production. It might be more logical to see banking not as one system but as two: local banks which integrated into the credit-circuit of merchants and manufacturers (see Section 2.9) and which to a great extent made up their own rules, and the central banking system, whose business traditionally lay in other directions, and which contributed usefully but only indirectly to economic expansion.

How did it do so? You would see from Crouzet that in France, which had no central bank, economic expansion was no less rapid between 1715 and 1789 than in England. But the Bank was useful in creating a class of fundholders, creditors of the government, whose position – unlike that of their continental counterparts – was guaranteed and secure. This social role was probably more significant than any directly economic benefits which accrued. Ashton's point about the role of the central banks in transferring cash from agriculture to industry is not really borne out by the facts – agricultural profits tended to go directly into a distinct but no less important field – transport improvement. Moreover, the role of the banks in manufacturing industry has subsequently been reinterpreted. Ashton's conclusion was that they had only advanced short-term loans: recent research has shown that such loans tended to be extended into loans of considerable duration. The local bank was thus an essential link in the chain of credit on which the expansion of manufacturing industry was based.

Figure 35   John Wilkinson's coinage

Section 2.11
The Businessmen

Preliminary reading
Ashton pp. 9–17, 76–87
Hobsbawm pp. 54, 58–9, 71–2
(*Industrialisation and Culture D1, D2*)

Introduction

I have decided to open this section with an extended radio supplement dealing with the Unit 6 radio broadcast 'Wilkinson the Iron King'. This should serve

to introduce you to some of the relationships we shall study in greater detail
later. If, for any reason, you can't get the broadcast, you'll find my procedure
more roundabout but you should get the gist of my meaning.

The broadcast

First of all, I hope you'll use the broadcast to compare the career of an actual
eighteenth-century industrialist with Ashton's and Hobsbawm's treatment of
entrepreneurship in their respective books. The questions are designed to help
you to do this.

EXERCISE

Of the questions which follow, you will find it necessary to jot down answers
to (1) during the broadcast, but you should be able to do the rest afterwards.

1   Throughout his career Wilkinson was dependent on a variety of sources
for finance. Note down as many as you think are mentioned in the programme, and whether you consider these were typical or untypical of most
businessmen of the time.

2   John Wilkinson was educated at the Reverend Caleb Rotherham's Uni-
tarian academy at Kendal. Can you suggest two ways in which this was
significant?

3   The iron-making empire of the Wilkinsons expanded rapidly in the late
1750s, but Isaac came unstuck in the early 1760s.
Suggest a reason
(a)   why this happened
and
(b)   why John and William avoided the same fate.

4   (a)   Can you think of one reason why an empire as widely dispersed as
Wilkinson's was possible in the latter part of the eighteenth century?
(b)   Besides the works connected with the iron manufacture Wilkinson
owned, or had shares in, potteries, collieries, lime kilns, agricultural estates
and copper and lead mines. Can you suggest a reason for his ownership of
these?
Wilkinson purchased the estates of Brymbo and Castle Head.
(c)   What was the difference between the two purchases?
(d)   Bearing in mind the activities of his contemporaries, what would your
comment be on his purchase of Castle Head?

5   There follow several descriptions some of which may be applicable to
Wilkinson as a businessman. I want you to underline 'agree' or 'disagree'
in each case, and state your reasons.
(a)   Wilkinson was a brilliant inventor who prospered through the successful application of his innovations.

        agree   disagree

(b)   Wilkinson's career showed him an impeccable free-trader, liberal
and internationalist.

        agree   disagree

(c)   Wilkinson was a typical businessman of the period of the Industrial
Revolution, grasping, unscrupulous, amoral.

        agree   disagree

(d)   Wilkinson's talent was less for invention than for adapting and making
effective relatively slight innovations of his own and the greater products
of others.

        agree   disagree

SPECIMEN ANSWER

Here are my own responses to these questions.

1 typical sources of finance	(a) salary as manager to a company (b) money advanced for raw materials
untypical sources of finances	(c) money from heiresses he married (d) money possibly obtained by fraud (e) money from the exploitation of a new invention

2(a) The Unitarians were a significant non-conformist group, active in industry and trade.
  (b) Dissenting schools tended to give good instruction in the sort of skills which made for success in industry.

3(a) Iron making expanded rapidly in the war years then slumped when peace came.
  (b) We can only guess, but John's second marriage to an heiress may have given them enough cash to tide them over.

4(a) Improvements in transport, notably the canals, had by this time connected up the areas in which he was interested.
  (b) One reason could be to supply the raw materials for iron manufacture – limestone and coal as well as ironstone; another could be a wish to diversify his interests in the event of a slump in the highly unstable iron trade.
  (c) Brymbo was purchased for industrial purposes, for its mines and works; Castle Head was owned, almost created, as a recreation.
  (d) It was fairly common for industrialists to buy estates to retire to.

  5 My own choice would be to *disagree* with all apart from (d).

DISCUSSION

I have used John Wilkinson as an example to illustrate the qualities which made for success in eighteenth-century business. Before we discuss these in detail I would like you to go over Ashton's and Hobsbawm's treatments of the entrepreneurs.

EXERCISE

1 Which is the more complex explanation, and why?
2 Which writer is more favourably disposed to the entrepreneurs?
3 Do you notice a difference in the number of industries Ashton and Hobsbawm deal with?
4 Do you see any reason for Hobsbawm's choice?

SPECIMEN ANSWER

  1 Ashton's is the more complex explanation: while Hobsbawm is content to see the entrepreneur as a man able to make a small amount of capital or credit go a long way in favourable circumstances, Ashton lays stress on the special religious, educational and scientific background from which many of the greatest eighteenth-century businessmen emerged.

2   Ashton: because he credits them with having coped with a more difficult adaptation of factors of production, he naturally credits them with having earned the rewards that certainly accrued to them. Although Hobsbawn sees them as an inevitable development he does not absolve them from responsibility for the deficiencies and hardships caused by industrialization.

3   Hobsbawm basically confines himself to the cotton industry, while Ashton ranges over practically all the industries affected by technical change in the period 1760–1830.

4   Hobsbawm features the cotton industry because he sees this as the 'leading sector' of the industrialization process.

DISCUSSION

As indicated in 3 and 4 above, Hobsbawm has tended to concentrate on the area of really vast expansion. In terms of the classical Marxist interpretation of the function of the businessmen in accumulating capital, this is straightforward enough: as you've seen from Section 2.5 the mechanization of the textile industry was technically a simple process and the getting of fixed and working capital (Section 2.9) didn't involve any great innovations in business organization. So, here at least, it seems that Ashton's more elaborate treatment is superfluous: no great qualities of character, religious background, scientific knowledge, were necessary to make a man a cotton king. A spinner working as a sub-contractor on the putting-out system might manage to save enough in a good year to buy a jenny, thus step up and cheapen production, buy his own cotton on credit, sell yarn at a profit, buy more jennies, then some frames to put in a rented water mill. Given a few good years, he might become a master spinner worth several thousand.

EXERCISE

This seems to give the impression that almost anyone could become a master spinner. Why do you think only a relatively few made it?

SPECIMEN ANSWER

A considerable element of risk was involved. The spinner made it if trade held up. But a depression could easily break the cycle of credit and force him into bankruptcy.

DISCUSSION

The risks involved must have deterred many journeymen spinners. This would have been attributed by the Victorians to their lack of independence and moral fibre, but at the time, with good wages to be made in weaving, there cannot have been all that much enthusiasm for 'going it alone'. As I have mentioned earlier, for the survivors the rewards were enormous, but subsequently they tended to dwindle as the industry reached saturation point in the 1830s.

In the second wave of industrialization, about to break only at the end of our period, entrepreneurship was more complex. The railway emerged from industries – iron, coal, engineering – which might not have had the *economic* importance of the cotton industry, but in the long term were *technically* more significant. And here the qualities of the businessmen involved in them seem to have been of a higher order: Wilkinson, for instance, may not have been an inventor of the first rank, but he knew how to use the inventions of others, how to delegate responsibility, how to take advantage of improvements in transport. Watt, who was an inventor of genius, also had these qualities, as had Stephenson.

In the case of these three, success wasn't simple, nor did their individual efforts call new industries into being, but they were conscious of relatively long-term possibilities, which brought in their train technical and organizational problems to be overcome. It is a delicate matter to decide to what extent these men made their industry, and to what extent it made them, but what I can say is that, to me, Hobsbawm's pattern of entrepreneurship seems true for textiles, while Ashton's is valid for the metal, mineral and chemical industries which were later to take the lead.

This leads me to reinterpret certain of the factors Ashton adduces in support of his case:

1   First religion: it is difficult to prove any correlation between religious belief and industrial success. One of the drawbacks of what has been done so far in this field has been the tendency to lump together all those who were not members of the Church of England as 'non-conformists' and forget that under this heading there were violent theological and organizational divisions. Ashton tends to do this on page 14, where it would be more apposite to point out the heterodoxy of his list, as well as the fact that major industrialists like Arkwright and Peel were loyal Anglicans.

What religion did do in certain instances, notably the Quakers, was to provide evidence of reliability and a network of contacts throughout the country. When, for instance, a Quaker banker, Samuel Pease, was promoting the Stockton and Darlington Railway in the early 1820s, he was able to call on other Friends for assistance, as far away as Norwich and London.

In other cases, a common dissenting religion may have provided a certain unity of interest between master and man, helping to ameliorate tension in labour relations: especially in the case of the more fundamentalist sects.

The opposite could be the case, when a dissenting religion like unitarianism approached close to the deism of the international liberal community. Joseph Priestley, John Wilkinson's brother-in-law, was closer to Lavoisier in France and Jefferson in America than he was to the Birmingham workmen who wrecked his house and laboratory in 1791 (see Hobsbawm p. 220).

2   Scientific advance penetrated most deeply at this rather exalted level (see Section 2.6): the men who introduced French chemical processes into bleaching and dyeing – largely into Scotland – were in the main professional men like Dr. John Roebuck or James Watt. Yet, as we have seen, up to the end of our period such scientific advances were of only limited importance.

3   Which brings us to education: again, in a period when the theoretical basis of technical advance was secondary to the practical, this was not of the greatest importance – George Stephenson was illiterate, and although he sent his son Robert to Edinburgh University, which had then the highest reputation of any university in the kingdom for a modern curriculum, Robert was not impressed. The workshop of a skilled craftsman was always the main schoolroom for the engineer.

Finally, I want to look briefly at two further sources of recruitment to the ranks of the industrial businessmen. First, there are the more or less traditional merchants who moved into manufacturing. David Dale of New Lanark cotton mills invested profits in the Atlantic trade in a cotton mill, and both John Wilkinson and Robert Owen, Dale's successor at New Lanark, had started as retail merchants. One plausible reason for the move from trade into industry was the fact that bankrupt businesses were most likely to fall into the hands of merchants as creditors, who might then proceed to run them.

A second channel was the exploitation of agriculture: not only did many land-owners have mines, quarries and mills on their estates, but over the preceding century they had evolved a functionary to look after them – a land agent. The creation of an equivalent role in manufacturing industry – the modern profes-sional manager – was a lengthy process, still incomplete at the end of our period, but the land agent was well fitted to take over the role of entrepreneur. William James, the early patron of George Stephenson, was an extensive landowner as well as agent, and possessed several collieries and an engineering practice as well.

Summing-up: invention and innovation

At the beginning of Part 2 I asked you to compare Ashton and Hobsbawm's views of the nature of innovation in industry over our period. We then went on to look at the process of innovation, business by business. At this stage it is worth returning to our original discussion, and try to sum up in general the degree of scientific and technological advance required, and the degree of organization and business adaptation.

By and large, the impression I derive from a detailed study of the course of technological and organizational change is one of the adaptation and, within limits, the extension of *existing knowledge* to a set of problems posed by more general economic changes. So in studying *why* industry changed, as opposed to *how* it changed, I feel we have to look at the social and economic context which both required and facilitated such adaptations.

I would tend myself to put most weight on *early* agricultural expansion. This seems to have produced both higher real incomes and a more efficient industry. This meant that the part-time employment of farm hands in textiles, the backbone of the 'putting-out' system, was less practicable, and that a substitute for human effort in textiles had to be found. Rising real incomes at this period meant that demand rose, both for food, which reinforced agricultural growth, and for clothes – next to food the most significant item of consumption. Such a demand pressed on the relatively inflexible supplies of wool and linen, and increased the attractiveness of cotton as a substitute.

The combination of a growth in demand with a likely crisis in labour supply led to the successful use of mechanized processes which had been for some time at an experimental stage. The success of these and the consciousness of the potent combination of steeply falling production costs and an expanding market abroad was sufficient to start the dramatic rise in production which was a feature of the 1780s.

The other industries were traditionally smaller in scale than agriculture and textiles. However, even a modest increase in demand brought about problems. Elsewhere these might have caused a halt to growth but, with expansion in two major sectors of the economy, such problems had inevitably to be tackled. I think it can fairly be argued that the resolution of the development difficulties of the industries which were the lines of *secondary expansion* – notably coal and iron – both required a higher level of innovation and provided the basis for subsequent industrial growth.

Whose side, then, do I come down on? It is really rather difficult to say. The technology which contributed to the expansion of the major industrial sector 'of the economy – the textile industry – was undoubtedly a relatively simple one, which aligns me with Hobsbawm on that issue. The impression given by Ashton, of a massing of technical and organizational expertise, ready to descend on and remould industry in general in 1760 is not, I think, a totally accurate one. Industries came to their 'critical points' at different times, and increasingly reacted to the general economic change caused by the rise of factory-produced textiles.

On the other hand, I would judge the background to the industrialization of the eighteenth century to be that of an expanding domestic market, not, as Hobsbawm seems to indicate, predominantly an export market. This conclusion conflicts with the Marxist model, as I find it difficult to see, in a rising home demand, a decline in the standard of living of the mass of the people. I tend to think that Hobsbawm's concentration on the export market reflects a certain unwillingness to admit that, during the run-up to the expansion at the end of the eighteenth century, working-class living standards had actually improved. Whether in the more mature industrial community of the early nineteenth century they continued to do so is a vexed question, and one to which we shall turn in Part 3.

PART 3

CONSEQUENCES

This part concerns the consequences of the first phase of industrialization. We have already examined the role of landowners and capitalists in some detail, so I've dealt fairly briefly with them, reserving most of my space for a study of the experience of the working class.

Section 3.1
The Landed Classes

Preliminary reading
Hobsbawm pp. 48–9, 180–201 (do not read in detail)
(*Industrialisation and Culture* B1)

EXERCISE

From what you've studied up to now, what elements of economic change do you think the owners of land would benefit from? Here are four individuals, each connected with land in his own way, whom you will find in the index to Ashton and Hobsbawm. I want you to specify, in each case, the connection with industrial progress (in the broadest sense) you associate with each.
1   Coke of Holkham
2   Lord Dundonald
3   The Duke of Bridgwater
4   John Wilkinson

SPECIMEN ANSWER

1   Improvements in agricultural techniques, bringing about higher productivity and consequently higher rents (Section 2.1).
2   The exploitation of the minerals on his estates (Section 2.2).
3   Investment in 'public utilities' like canals and turnpikes (Section 2.8).
4   The exploitation by the manufacturing and commercial interests of land for reasons of industry and status.

DISCUSSION

The first three categories are relatively straightforward and there is not really much need to discuss them further. They are evidence that in Britain the integration between the rational exploitation of land and capital was close. The fourth is less straightforward but confirms this.

Now I want to discuss in rather more detail another factor, linked to some extent with 4. We must remember that until the 1860s the structure of government in Britain, thought not its programme, was aristocratic (see Section 2.1). Aristocratic influence also reigned in the Church, Oxford and Cambridge, the Civil Service and the armed services. We will discuss the Reform Bill of 1832 in greater detail in Unit 8, but bear in mind that it was not a victory for the business classes so much as for a wing – the Whigs – of the landed interest. The Whigs gained power by virtue of urban agitation, and maintained it by acting as the 'avocati' (the pleaders) – as Marx put it – for the business class. But it is difficult to imagine them retaining this ascendancy without the strength brought about by economic change. We should also be rather critical of Hobsbawm when he sees the landed classes as protectionist. This is probably true of the farmers but not of their landlords, who had a variety of investment options open to them. They could afford, for political reasons, to lend support to the cry for free trade. The farmers, by and large, could not, and voted for Tories pledged against the repeal of the Corn Laws.

The close linkage strengthened industry, too. If anything it became closer at the end of our period with the growth of railway investment, which was much favoured by aristocratic investors whose fathers had backed transport improvement schemes, and also by the banking interest, the most respectable part of the commercial world, which was increasingly aristocratic in its life-style.

You may find it interesting to look up the history of landed families in your neighbourhood, and see what sort of impact the economic changes of this period had on them: for instance, in the area near the Open University we have the Duke of Bedford at Woburn Abbey, a typical 'improving landlord' of the time, with enclosure programmes, plantations, model villages, and so on, but also with a substantial income deriving from his London property in the Bloomsbury area. Then at Waddesdon and Tring are the properties of the Rothschilds, the Jewish merchant bankers, and Wolverton provided a title for George Carr Glyn, the banker and chairman of the London and North Western Railway, whose main line was built through the district in 1838. (It's worth noting that all three families were at this time Liberal in their politics.)

Section 3.2
The Capitalist Classes and the Problems of the Industrial Economy

Preliminary reading
Hobsbawm pp. 58–63, 218–37
Ashton pp. 114–29
(*Industrialisation and Culture* D2, E1, H2)

The period after the Napoleonic Wars was one in which the textile industry, the 'leading sector' of the British economy, reached a stage of fairly complete mechanization (see Section 2.5, p. 49). At the end of this period, between 1830, when the Liverpool and Manchester Railway (*Industrialisation and Culture* E1) opened and about 1843, when the great railway boom got underway, a restructuring of the economy was taking place, away from the production of consumer goods and towards the production of 'capital goods' (Hobsbawm pp. 62–3). This in its turn created a new wave of industrialization whose implications are dealt with quite adequately by Hobsbawm, and by me in A100 Units 29–30.

However, this transition was by no means a rapid or a smooth process, and its history reveals, I think, certain immaturities in the development of industrial capitalism at this period.

First of all, I feel we must look in some detail at the main phenomenon of this period, which is the punctuation of economic continuity by periods of depression. You may recollect that Ashton notes (p. 118) how the production of bricks reflects the course of the economy. So here is a graph of this, 1800–30.

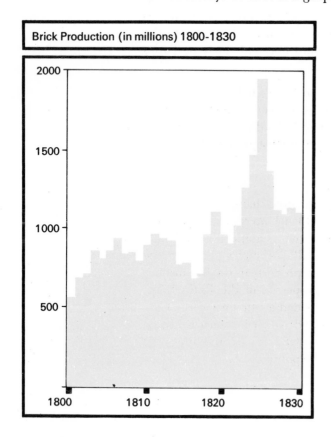

Figure 36

EXERCISE

1   What periods of boom and slump do you identify?
2   Where would you draw a dividing line in the history of the period?

SPECIMEN ANSWER

> 1   There's a boom in the mid-1800s, a slump thereafter, then a boom in
> the 1810 period followed by a bad slump around 1815, a big boom in
> the mid-1820s and a sharp slump thereafter.
> 2   You could take the end of the Napoleonic war in 1815 as a dividing
> line.

DISCUSSION

Here we have two main periods, both disfigured by economic instability, and
the social disorganization and political disturbance which accompanied it.

EXERCISE

1   What reasons does Ashton give for the economic difficulties of Britain
between 1800 and 1830?
2   What is Hobsbawm's explanation?

SPECIMEN ANSWER

> Ashton
> 1   Lays stress on:
>   (a) the disruptive effect of the war;
>   (b) the slowness of the government to adapt itself to running an
>   industrial society;
>   (c) the effect of depressions induced by harvest failure.

> Hobsbawm
> 2   Lays stress on:
>   (a) the effect of cyclical depressions;
>   (b) the declining rate of profit in cotton manufacture;
>   (c) the failure of the cost of living to fall, and so lower wages.

DISCUSSION

Now, distinguishing between the two interpretations, Hobsbawm looks *within*
the capitalist class itself, whereas Ashton is more concerned to explain it with
reference to *external* factors. This, of course, affects the record of the capitalists
themselves. Were they inhibited from breaking out of this situation because
of their inability to take a wider view of society and of wealth, or did they have
the answers but were prevented from applying them by the inertia of established
institutions and government policy?

War and the economy

We discussed the role of the wars of the eighteenth century in stimulating
British industrialization then: was there any appreciable difference between
their effect and that of the Napoleonic war?

In fact, the war had a more explicitly economic side than its predecessors:
Britain blockaded France from 1793–1815, and France made a determined
effort to cut off British exports by the 'Continental System' of 1808–12.

EXERCISE

What were the effects of this:
(a)   according to Ashton;
(b)   according to Hobsbawm?

SPECIMEN ANSWER

> According to both, the blockades did have a critical effect, especially during the period of mutual blockade, 1808–12. But, Hobsbawm argues, basically Britain benefited through the blockade, as she thus captured markets from her European rivals.

DISCUSSION

In an article published in the *Journal of Economic History*, 1964, François Crouzet argued that the British blockade severely damaged the industries which subsisted around the French ports – shipbuilding, sugar refining, distillers, glassworks, sail and rope-making, boilermaking, and so on – which made them, in Crouzet's opinion, 'undoubtedly the most industrialized in the eighteenth century'. The damage the counter-blockade did to British industry was proportionately less – although it did have an effect on the bad British slump after 1808 – and Britain secured from France a leading role in South America which was to become a major export market. I think this can be seen as partially offsetting the economic slump which accompanied the end of the war, and, of course, putting Britain into a stronger position *vis à vis* her continental rivals.

Peace and instability

As you can see from Figure 36, the aftermath of the war saw wild fluctuations in the economy. These continued until the 1840s, when there was, under the aegis of railway development, a long and sustained upswing. We have noted Ashton's and Hobsbawm's interpretations of these difficulties. I would like to give here my own.

If the home market for consumer goods was not rising, because of the slow increase in the prosperity of the mass of the people, then it was difficult to provide another mass-consumption industry to invest in, since the market for it didn't exist. Investment thus tended either to be ploughed back into the textile industry or to go into unstable schemes of foreign investment; both tended to increase the economic instability of the time, and the risk of disastrous depressions.

We'll discuss the standard of living of the industrial work force later, in Section 3.3. By and large, as will be apparent from the foregoing, I accept Hobsbawm's approach. My reservations are that I don't find the case for actual *deterioration* of living standards proved, and that I would lay special stress on the difficulty that faced British capitalists of finding a substitute activity for investment to the textile industry. Such a problem was a very complex one: what I have said about the cotton industry showed its practically infinite capacity for expansion at very low cost. Can we say the same about later growth industries – food processing, mass-produced clothing and furniture, and so forth?

Now you may remember that in A100 Units 29–30 we saw the necessity of *prior transport change* for the creation of the consumer-orientated industries of the later nineteenth century. Rapidity of communication was so obviously the key to further expansion that the railway was virtually an inevitable choice. Why then did it take so long to get it under way?

Well, partly this delay was due to technical reasons (Section 2.8). It was not until 1830 that the railway was technically superior in all respects to competing forms of transport. But there was also a lack of inventiveness and foresight on the part of the suppliers and manipulators of capital. After all, it is a pretty poor reflection on the most advanced industrial society in Europe, that the innovation which essentially sustained its growth was the work of semi-literate mechanics, arrived at by a more or less haphazard process of trial and error. Could a sophisticated class of scientists and engineers, educated to appreciate its problems, not have speeded up innovation and the restructuring of the economy, and eliminated much of the dislocation?

Hobsbawm takes this line, and argues that the growth of such a class was militated against by the capitalist class itself. It devoted itself so ruthlessly to making money through a relatively simple technology that it hadn't the time for the cultivation of values which were essential in the long term in a practical as well as a cultural sense.

British capitalism was not merely grasping: its greed made it stupid, and its stupidity made it unadaptable. There is a great deal of truth in this: throughout the nineteenth century British industry was dogged by an unthinking conservatism of method which impeded progress. However this isn't, I feel, the whole truth. Cotton manufacturers may have been unwilling to innovate, but this wasn't because they were greedy to the exclusion of foresight. The careers of Robert Owen and John Fielden, who combined being very substantial cotton magnates with zeal for social reform, showed that effort could be directed in other directions besides making money. And the existence of civil engineers and architects of high quality – Smeaton, Telford, Rennie, the Adam brothers – who worked for commercial concerns shows that industrial requirements didn't extinguish talent.

What seems apparent is that the minds of British capitalists were moulded by the structure of the industries in which their wealth was made. The mechanization of the textile industry was a relatively simple process: its integration into the rest of the economy involved some major break throughs – organizational rather than technical – at the time but, once stability was achieved, relatively little continuous innovatory activity. We could almost say of the British capitalists between 1800 and 1830 what Crouzet said of the French economy in the mid eighteenth century: they didn't challenge themselves and were content to produce more of the same. When the challenge came, through recurrent economic crises, they responded in an unsystematic and opportunist manner. They were successful, but their continental rivals were able to make note of their mistakes, and plan to avoid them.

Section 3.3
The Working Class

Preliminary reading
Hobsbawm pp. 57–61, 238–57
Ashton pp. 88–101, 106–13, 114–29
(A100 Unit 8, pp. 32–59, essays on the standard of living of working people during the Industrial Revolution, by E. J. Hobsbawm and R. M. Hartwell; *Industrialisation and Culture* A1, B3, C5, 6, Section F, G1, 3, 5.)

Introduction

The question whether the standard of living of the labouring classes rose or fell between 1760 and the mid 1840s – when it certainly started to rise – is, of all the controversies which centre on our period, the hardest fought. Significantly enough, Arthur Marwick uses it to illustrate 'Controversy in History' in the broadcast accompanying A100 Unit 8, with E. J. Hobsbawm and R. M. Hartwell as proponents of, respectively, the 'pessimistic' and the 'optimistic' approaches to the problem. The broadcast, and the essays by Hobsbawm and Hartwell, are worth attention if you want a more detailed treatment. In this section, however, I intend to confine myself to Ashton's and Hobsbawm's treatment in the set books.

EXERCISE

1 After reading the set extracts from Ashton and Hobsbawm, how would you define, in the broadest terms, the 'optimist' and 'pessimist' positions.
2 What sort of attitude does each position imply to the 'laissez-faire' economy of the time?
3 Can you see any connection between such attitudes and the politics of the present day?

SPECIMEN ANSWER

> 1 Broadly speaking, the 'optimist' sees industrialization leading to a higher standard of life, the 'pessimist' to a deterioration.
>
> 2 The 'optimist' believes that capitalism will, without intervention by government, lead to growth *and* increasing prosperity for the mass of society. The 'pessimist' can cite the experience of unrestricted capitalism as a condemnation of its performance.
>
> 3 At the present day advocates of a 'free market' economy are likely to be found in the ranks of the optimists, while socialists – or those committed to government intervention in the economy, are likely to be found on the 'pessimist' side.

DISCUSSION

The debate over the standard of living has thus a significance which is as much political as academic. You may remember that in Section 1.1 (p. 10) I pointed out the costs and benefits of such controversy. The warning is worth repeating here; as this particular engagement seems to have generated rather more heat than light.

I've already mentioned that my own views imply a qualified acceptance of Hobsbawm's position (Section 3.2, p. 78). However, in this section I'm less concerned to expatiate on his or Ashton's or my own conclusions than to get you to identify from the controversy the main areas at which we will have to look to understand the impact which, for good or ill, industrialization had on the mass of the population.

EXERCISE

I want you to go through Section II (pp. 243–48) of Hobsbawm's Chapter 11, 'The Labouring Poor', and note down ten headings which represent areas of research Hobsbawm has explored. (For instance, you can class the information at the bottom of p. 243 as derived from *economic theory and opinion*, and so on.)

SPECIMEN ANSWER

> 1   Economic theory and opinion
> 2   Records of harvest and famine
> 3   Examination of 'real incomes'
> 4   History of urban government
> 5   History of food supply
> 6   Urban health studies
> 7   Studies of depressions and resulting unemployment
> 8   Studies of unemployment caused by industrial change
> 9   Studies of working conditions
> 10 Studies of working-class opinion

DISCUSSION AND EXERCISE

Now I don't intend to discuss all these in detail, but what I will do, with each of the ten, is to give you a paraphrase of an opinion on or from that 'source' from either the Ashton or the Hobsbawm side, and ask you (a) to say who it comes from and (b) how the other writer would combat it.

1 'That the condition of the labouring poor was appalling between 1815 and 1848 was not denied by any reasonable observer, and by 1840 there were a good many of these.'

         Ashton   (Hobsbawm)

2 Although agricultural improvements prevented serious famine, a bad harvest could still bring economic depression and unemployment.

         (Ashton)   Hobsbawm

3 Indices of real wages cannot be drawn with any real pretension to accuracy.

         Ashton   (Hobsbawm)

4 'In spite of the efforts of Thomas Percival and James Watt, the skies over Manchester and Birmingham grew dark with smoke, and life in the cities became drab. The smaller industrial towns, like Oldham or Bilston, had a harsh countenance: towns, to be good, should grow slowly.'

         (Ashton)   Hobsbawm

5 Finding out what people actually spent their money on, and how much there was of it to go round, seems to indicate that supplies were not keeping pace with demand.

         Ashton   (Hobsbawm)

6 The average expectation of life at birth in the 1840s was twice as high for the labourers of rural Wiltshire and Rutland than for those of Manchester or Liverpool.

         Ashton   (Hobsbawm)

7 Unemployment was more severe between 1815–40 than before or after.

         Ashton   (Hobsbawm)

8 'Over the eighteenth century, the material well-being of the labourer in the woollen area of the South-west had indeed fallen, but that the lot of his fellow in the textile region of the North had steadily improved.'

         (Ashton)   Hobsbawm

9 'Even in the regions about London, Manchester and Birmingham there were men and women who toiled laboriously, without the aids that science and ingenuity had brought to their fellows in the factory, the forge and the mine.'

         (Ashton)   Hobsbawm

10 That 'standard of living' which can be mathematically calculated, does not provide us with a 'standard of life' which takes account of the subjective reactions to industrialization of those involved in it.

         Ashton   (Hobsbawm)

SPECIMEN ANSWER

> 1 *Hobsbawm*
> It would be possible to quote opinion from as many sources to argue for an increase in living standards.

2   *Ashton*
Yet even in industrialized Britain at the end of our period a cataclysm like the Irish famine was possible.

3   *Hobsbawm*
Is Hobsbawm not saying this because such real-wage indices as have been calculated disprove his thesis?

4   *Ashton*
Life in the cities was not just drab, but shorter and more miserable.

5   *Hobsbawm*
This is a valid enough approach, but we have to remember that both diets and the way in which food was supplied changed a great deal at this time.

6   *Hobsbawm*
If death-rates declined, then the health of the population must have improved during industrialization. It can be argued that in aggregate, over this period, they did decline.

7   *Hobsbawm*
Was unemployment worse at this time than before or since? Hobsbawm does little to prove this.

8   *Ashton*
Do we know that the number of people whose real incomes went up was, in fact, greater than those whose incomes declined?

9   *Ashton*
Factory labour may have been remunerative, but it was also taxing, monotonous, and frequently dangerous to the operative.

10   *Hobsbawm*
Can you deny with opinions what statistics establish? If the trend of real incomes was up then discontent was brought on more by expectation than by despair.

DISCUSSION

I don't propose to look at all these in detail: 7 we dealt with when looking at capital and the responsibility for economic depression, 2 when studying banking, and 6 in Section 1, when discussing population change. 9 you should be able to judge for yourself by the industries featured in Section 2.

I want now to deal with 3, 5 and 8 – which are concerned with statistical interpretations of change. Then I want to go on to discuss 1 – the opinions on the condition of labour of the 'respectable classes' and 4, the actions taken by central and local government, finally ending up with 10, labour's own interpretation of its position.

Indices of real wages

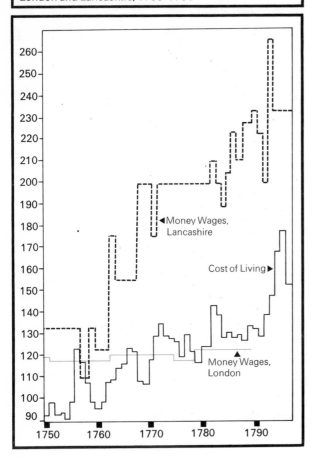

| Indices of Money-Wages and Cost of Living Indices |
| London and Lancashire, 1750-1796 |

Figure 37

This diagram shows the *indices* of money-wages – that is, the cash a workman is paid each week – for workmen in London and Lancashire, and for the cost of living *in London* at the time. An 'index of prices or wages' is a simple way of comparing various figures much used by economic historians. The wage of one year – in this case 1700 – is called a hundred per cent, and those of other years are reduced to percentage terms above or below the original figure. An index number of 125, for instance, means an increase of twenty-five per cent, seventy-five a decrease of twenty-five per cent and so on.

EXERCISE

1   When you compare the rise or fall of money wages with the rise or fall of prices, what would you call the result?
2   In this respect, how does London compare with Lancashire over this period?
3   How would you explain this?
4   Look at the years 1756–8: how do you explain the position of the various indices then?
5   Can you point to years where the opposite seems to be the case, and explain what the economic reasons for the position of the indices might have been?
6   What drawbacks do you see to this particular diagram in calculating the 'real wages' of Lancashire?
7   How would you make up a cost-of-living index?

SPECIMEN ANSWERS

> I
>
> This comparison should give the level of increase or decrease of 'real wages' – which in turn give us an idea of the 'standard of living'.

DISCUSSION

Indices like these are still used to calculate the 'cost of living' today.

When we hear a news bulletin mention that the 'cost of living' has gone up two points, this is what it means – in fact it is usually referred to as the 'retail price index'.

> 2
>
> In London the level of real wages appears to have gone down, in Lancashire it went up.
>
> 3
>
> A possible explanation might be that, living in a hitherto thinly populated area which became a textile centre, Lancashire people found their labour was in short supply, and were able to insist on higher wages. Further, London was, as a city, a place to which those forced off the land by improvement and enclosure would naturally gravitate, thus holding down wage levels by swelling the supply of labour.
>
> 4
>
> In 1756–8 wage indices in Lancashire fall, cost-of-living indices rise: (Ashton, p. 117) a couple of bad harvests increased food costs, lost money in foreign exchange for imports, thus diverting it from industry, causing unemployment and lower wages (see Section 3.2).
>
> 5
>
> The opposite seems to happen in 1768–70, when wages rise and costs fall. We would expect to find at this time good harvests, 'cheap money' and booming exports.
>
> 6
>
> The drawback is the absence of a cost-of-living index for Lancashire. Might not an increase in demand have increased prices as well as wages?

DISCUSSION

On the face of it, Lancashire workers seem to be doing well throughout this period, but until we know the cost of living for Lancashire, we really can't tell how well. And, for reasons I'll go into later in more detail, this may prove a very difficult task.

> 7
>
> A cost-of-living index is obviously made up of the cost to the individual of the food, clothing, rent etc., needed to keep him in subsistence.

DISCUSSION

You can see examples of such an index in Clive Emsley's breakdown of a French worker's expenditure, 1700-1800 (Unit 1, p. 21).

The first British attempt to relate prices to wages was made in the middle of the nineteenth century by Thorold Rogers, the Professor of Economics at Oxford. As one source for prices he used the account-books of the colleges. Such institutional records have been a major source for prices, because they have continuity and system which few other sources – families for instance – exhibit.

On the other hand, in some respects institutions like Oxford or Cambridge are not wholly representative – they tended to be in the south of England, to have considerable interrelationships with the land, which may have meant that they bought at lower cost than the individual would have done. Also they bought for a number of people – dons and students, for instance – and bought in bulk and wholesale. All of these can be considered distorting factors.

We must also bear in mind that the various components of the cost-of-living index have to be put together.

Here, for instance, is the cost-of-living index compiled by Dr. N. J. Silberling which Ashton used (p. 127).[1]

Food (42 points):		Clothing (8 points):	
Wheat	15	Wool	3
Mutton	6	Cotton	3
Beef	6	Flax	1
Butter	5	Leather	1
Oats	3		
Sugar	3		
Coffee	1		
Tobacco	1		
Tea	2		
Fuel and Light (6):		Total 56 points	
Coal	4		
Tallow	2		

You'll notice that Silberling doesn't include either rent or beer, which makes for a pretty odd picture of the working man of this or any period. Moreover, and this is a failing of most indices, what he said was true only for some workers in some places. The differences which we noticed, for example, between London and Lancashire were repeated throughout the country. In time, satisfactory real wage indices may be drawn up, trade by trade, but this will be a long process. It is not made any easier by the considerable structural changes in industries over this period, raising or lowering the wages of specific groups (like, for example, the handloom weavers whose wages fell with mechanization, and journeymen engineers, whose wages rose), and by the large variety of ways of paying wages (payment for piece-work, by sub-contract, to the boss or 'butty' of a gang of men, or to fathers whose families also worked). I would treat indices of wages with caution, although I would not go as far as Hobsbawm in rejecting them.

Calculating the standard of living through consumption

We have already looked at what the working man needed to live on when we examined the basis of Silberling's cost-of-living index. Calculating the standard of living through consumption involves estimating the total amount of any of these various commodities available to the community over a particular period.

For instance, here is a graph showing the indices of the numbers of cattle and sheep killed at Smithfield, the traditional London meat market, between 1811 and 1851, as compared with the index of the population of London.

1 From Clapham, J. H. (1939) *An Economic History of Modern Britain*, Vol. 1, pp. 601-2, Cambridge University Press.

Number of Cattle and Sheep Killed between 1801-1851

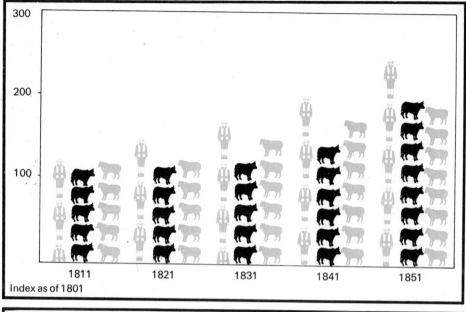

300

200

100

1811   1821   1831   1841   1851

Index as of 1801

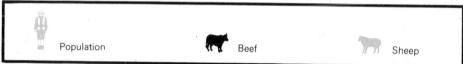

Population   Beef   Sheep

Figure 38

EXERCISE

1 What is the overall impression you get when you compare the movement of the population index to those of the livestock?
2 What does this indicate about the demand for, and the supply of, meat?
3 From this, how would you expect the price of meat to move?
4 What would the result be for the standard of living?

SPECIMEN ANSWER

> 1 The population index shows a faster rise than those of the livestock.

> 2 This indicates that the supply of meat rose slower than the demand for it.

> 3 The price of meat would obviously increase, as people will pay more to get a scarcer commodity.

> 4 In such circumstances the standard of living would certainly decline.

DISCUSSION

It would certainly decline unless money-wages were seen to be rising over the period as well. In fact, they were falling, or at best static. The old orthodoxy used to maintain that the cost of living was declining as well. If, because of the scarcity of foodstuffs in the new cities, it was not, then a plausible case for deterioration can be made out. The statistics here, appear to support this.

Against this, it has been argued that the graph mentions only cattle and sheep, not pigs, which were a staple part of the working-class diet, or fish, which was being eaten in greater quantity at this time. Further, Smithfield was not the only market in London; we can't generalize until we know about the others. (See the Hartwell article in A100 Unit 8 for an elaboration of these points.)

And of course we could also say that London was not Lancashire, and probably tended to attract a greater proportion of the very poor who came to beg rather than to work. And even among the poor, there seem to be some factors which lead to a belief that diet can't have been all that bad: look at the diet of Mayhew's sewer man (*Industrialisation and Culture* F9) and at the workhouses, where the diet, specifically intended to be less elaborate than that of the poorest employed labourer, nevertheless showed that a substantial amount of meat was served.

I think it's as difficult to generalize about consumption as about real wages. But I would say that, on Hobsbawm's side there remains an important argument. Until the railways came, and coastal steamers started to be used for freight transport, in the 1830s, the speed of freight transport had not increased much. This meant that getting dead meat, fish, fruit and vegetables into market in bulk was difficult. As town population increased, these had to be brought from greater distances, at greater cost. But more research is needed to determine the effect of transport change on the supply of food.

The attitude of informed opinion and government

Hobsbawm's argument is that even the supporters of liberal economics despaired at their effect on the mass of the population. There is a great deal of truth in this: John Stuart Mill the doyen of classical economists, in his *Principles of Political Economy* of 1848, doubted whether the use of machinery had materially improved the condition of the workman and, as late as the 1860s, Henry Fawcett, who was Professor of Economics at Cambridge and a Radical M.P. doubted whether the working classes could improve their position other than by limiting their numbers through late marriage or emigration.

EXERCISE

Whose hand do you see behind those gloomy conclusions, and why?

SPECIMEN ANSWER

> Malthus, who argued that an expanding population would always press on the means of subsistence: if income increased, population would as well.

DISCUSSION

Malthus was the wicked spirit at the christening of industrial Britain. In his *Essay on the Principal of Population* (1798) he argued that while the supply of food expanded in *arithmetical* progression (1,2,3,4) population grew in *geometrical* progression (2,4,6,8). The result could only be a static living standard for the mass of the population. This argument, seen against a background of rising population, economic crises, and urban squalor, may account for the fact, that in its rapid triumph, the Industrial Revolution was hymned by relatively few economists of the first rank, as it seemed to them to be going nowhere noisily and fast.

EXERCISE

Look at the passages about Manchester from De Tocqueville and Kay-Shuttleworth in *Industrialisation and Culture* (B3, F7.) The situation they deal with is depressing enough, but do you think it is as hopeless as the Malthusian attitude? If not, why not?

SPECIMEN ANSWER

> Both place much of the blame for the situation on the absence of public intervention and the resulting disorganization.

DISCUSSION

You will notice, if you compare two 'optimistic' accounts – Ashton and Hartwell's essay – that Ashton is sceptical of the impact of state interference, save in a negative sense, while Hartwell credits it with having contributed to the growing well-being of the working population. This reflects, I think, changes both in the theory of modern capitalism and in historical study of the early industrial period. In the first, after the adoption of Keynesian economic policies from the early 1940s on, and even earlier in the USA, economists became more sympathetic to the idea of the State playing a sustained and positive role in the economy, and were interested to estimate the effect of state intervention (or non-intervention) at earlier periods. Secondly, there has been a growing interest in Britain since the war in administrative history. Before then, the study of legislative change had concentrated on parliamentary action, but it became apparent that, during this period of great social change, much of the public action to cope with it came at a local level, local authorities, *ad hoc* public bodies, voluntary organizations and individuals who were prepared quite literally to take the law into their own hands, like Kay-Shuttleworth himself.

At the end of our period, in the Manchester cholera epidemic of 1832, the Poor Law enquiry of 1834 and the Sanitary Report of 1842, we have the first activities of that Victorian giant, Edwin Chadwick. You will find the conclusions of his Sanitary Report in *Industrialisation and Culture* (G3).

EXERCISE

I give below two paraphrases of Chadwick's position. Which do you think is the more accurate?

1   Sanitation is bad because market forces have not been allowed to work to secure a reasonable system by the decisions of independent individuals. The remedy is to allow such local and individual initiatives to operate.

2   In an ideal world, market forces should be allowed to determine the allocation of 'social investment', but the situation is potentially if not actually so disastrous that the only way out is to take the provision of sanitation out of the competition of the market.

SPECIMEN ANSWER

> Unquestionably 2

DISCUSSION

The problem here is one of dislocation, of the misapplication of resources. While theoretically this can't automatically be blamed on the prevailing economic system, this has been its practical consequence, and the only way out seems to be through state intervention. The problem is not that the towns of the Industrial Revolution were drab (Ashton p. 126) but that they didn't work, and could only be made to work by radically changing the system itself, and replacing individual with collective responsibility.

Class-consciousness

The view the working classes held about their own condition is not, of course, merely evidence as to what, in material terms, that condition was. If the new labour force articulated the view that it had nothing in common with, and was being exploited by, capital, then it had arrived at a perception which would have a critical influence on its future role. It had become class-conscious, in the classic Marxist sense of the term. (For an example of this see Engels on trade unionism in *Industrialisation and Culture* G1.)

EXERCISE

1   Which of the two writers, Ashton or Hobsbawm, seems closer to Engels?
2   Which would be most likely to stress the diversity of working-class reactions to industrial organization?
3   Which would tend to lay stress on the fact that hostile reactions to industrialism come substantially from the older trades?
4   Does either writer see the organization of labour in 1830 as representing a mature response to industrial capitalism?

SPECIMEN ANSWER

1   Hobsbawm
2   Ashton
3   Ashton
4   Neither

DISCUSSION

1   As a Marxist, Hobsbawm could reasonably be supposed to agree with Engels, with this difference: Engels believed that the next commercial depression, after the time (1842) at which he was writing, would be the critical one. What went wrong Hobsbawm indicates on pp. 147 and 361. The English rode out the 1842 depression, then restructured their economy through the boom in railway investment. This boom continued to provide employment through the dark days of 1848, when English unrest failed to mesh with that of the continent. Thereafter her near-fatal dependence on one major industrialized sector was broken, and the confrontation between labour and capital altered in character and postponed.

2   Marx tended to make the industrialization of the cotton industry – the transition from 'manufacture' to 'machinofacture' the basis for this analysis of the developing structure of capitalist industrial society. Indeed, it captured the imagination of his contemporaries to an extent that it comes as a shock to learn that even in 1860 the majority of British workmen still worked in concerns employing seven men or less. Moreover, the types of industrial organization varied intensely. If you go back over our survey of the industrial transformation you can see that enormous differences existed between the ways in which people worked.

EXERCISE

What points of contrast would you notice between, for instance, a canal boatman and a textile operative and their way of work?

SPECIMEN ANSWER

The textile operative works:
1   with machinery
2   to a rigid timetable

3   under strict surveillance
4   in a situation divorced from his home.

Whereas the canal boatman's life is the opposite in all these aspects. Although an employee, he works (at his own speed with forces he can control) on his own, and carrying his own home along with him.

DISCUSSION

I don't mean to imply here that the boatman's life was better than that of the mill operative. He was paid less, lived in conditions which, if picturesque, were very cramped, and which didn't improve much over time. But his work situation was totally different although, like the textile operative, the industry in which he worked was heavily capitalized.

EXERCISE

You might find it useful to make a list of those occupations covered in Part 2 which were subject to a new work discipline and those which remained in a traditional pattern.

SPECIMEN ANSWER

Traditional	*New*
Agriculture	Iron
Coal	Textiles
Engineering	Chemicals
Canals	Pottery
Road Transport	Railways

DISCUSSION

This is a very rough division. Canals and road transport I've already explained. Engineering remained a craft, and spawned its own traditions; coal-mining, as we noticed, was not radically mechanized during our period, and preserved a destructive type of behaviour and consciousness. In agriculture, the relations of labourers with their employers were different, because of the experience of different types of farm, the division between regular and casual workers who came in at harvest time, the influence of tied houses, and the like.

Even on the other side the work experience of the railways was qualitatively quite different from that of the mills. The rules were every bit as rigid (see A100 Units 29–30) but the organization was more hierarchical, offered more chance of promotion, and to some, jobs which were intrinsically rewarding, interesting, and not particularly strenuous. The transition from farm labouring to work as a porter or platelayer on a country branch line, with relatively light duties, a house and a pension to look forward to, cannot have been resented by the many who made it.

I am not suggesting that class-consciousness didn't exist, or that variation in work-experience by itself can be used to argue for improvement. The example of deterioration on the grand scale – that of the hand-loom weavers – can, I think, fairly be put in the balance on the other side. But, if such deterioration occurred it was in an aggregate sense: which doesn't really help us much in understanding the nature of a varied and constantly changing labour force.

The implication of Ashton's attitude is that opposition to industrial capitalism is more the conservative reaction of old skills threatened by it than the positive opposition of the labour force it created, as Marx had envisaged. Against this Hobsbawm would argue that frequently these 'old skills' were enhanced by industrialism – like hand-loom weaving and sweat-shop tailoring – only to be thrown aside when it suited the industrialists. Hobsbawm also pays tribute to the high intellectual standing of the older industrial communities, which he sees as being crushed by later changes.

The dialogue of industrial change and community-consciousness is a complex one: hitherto privileged groups and their traditions play an important role in giving a vocabulary to rising groups. In his classic *The Making of the English Working Class* E. P. Thompson sees the evolution of class-consciousness in less rigidly economic terms than Hobsbawm. He lays stress on the use of the political language of the revolutionary period (discussed by Clive Emsley in Unit 4) initially by the journeymen of the skilled trades, then by the emergent industrial labour force. This working-class consciousness he sees as well developed by the 1820s and in bearing fruit in the Chartist movement of the 1820s and '30s, setting its face against the ideology of the commercial middle class not by a conservative opposition to innovation but by demanding a 'social control' over the way industry and the economy functioned.

Thompson sees the Reform agitation of 1830–32 as the critical period of agitation, when middle-class capitalists succeeded the aristocracy as the enemy of labour. Chartism followed, and, Thompson implies, the distinctive independence of British labour was thereafter transmitted to trade unions and the socialist movement.

I for one find this continuity difficult to accept, as does Hobsbawm, when he writes that 'by 1848 the movement of the labouring poor had yet to develop its equivalent to the Jacobinism of the revolutionary middle class of 1789–94'. The Chartist movement remained a political movement, not an industrial one. Its ideology was indeed that of the 1820s and 1830s, but is showed little sign of developing an analysis of revolutionary possibilities inherent in capitalist industry that Marx and Engels argued for. In fact, its course was closer to an automatic reflection of economic fluctuations, increasingly salted with the distinctive political ideology of the Irish, until, with the upswing of the 1850s and the restructuring of the economy by railways and their associated capital-goods industries, it withered. It gave way to a reaction to capitalist industry based much more closely on bargaining positions within specific industries, on craft trade unions of the 'new model' pattern and their associated trades councils and parliamentary contacts, actuarially 'sound' Co-ops and friendly societies. These implied an acceptance of the new industrial society coupled politically with a radical class loyalty which undoubtedly owed much to earlier experiences. It was, I think, only later, in the experience of a second and more critical economic depression, after 1870, that the British working class began to assume its familiar shape – with a mass trade-union movement and a parliamentary presence.

REFERENCES

Ashton, T. S. (1969) *The Industrial Revolution, 1760–1830*, Oxford University Press (set book).

Barker, T. C. (1960) 'The Beginning of the Canal Age' in Pressnell, L. S. (ed.) *Studies in the Industrial Revolution*, Athlone Press.

Crouzet, F. (1964) 'Wars, Blockade and Economic Change in Europe, 1792–1815', *Journal of Economic History*, vol. XXIV.

Crouzet, F. (1967) 'England and France in the eighteenth century: a comparative analysis of two economic growths', trans. I. Sondheimer, in Hartwell, R.M. (ed.) *The Causes of the Industrial Revolution*, Methuen.

Habbakkuk, H. J. (1953) 'English Population in the 18th Century', *Economic History Review*, 2nd series, vol. VI.

Harvie, C., Martin, G. and Scharf, A. (eds.) (1971) *Industrialisation and Culture*, The Open University Press/Macmillan (A100 Course Reader).

Hobsbawm, E. J. (1962) *The Age of Revolution*, Mentor/New English Library Ltd. (set book).

Lord, J. (1966) *Capital and Steam Power, 1750–1800*, Frank Cass and Co.

The Open University (1971) A100 Humanities: A Foundation Course, Unit 8 *Common Pitfalls in Historical Writing*, Units 29–30 *The Industrialisation Process 1830–1914*, Unit 31 *The Debate on Industrialisation*, The Open University Press.

Thompson, E. P. (1963) *The Making of the English Working Class*, Victor Gollancz.

Williams, M. (1971) (ed.) *Revolutions 1775–1830*, The Open University Press/Penguin Education (Course Reader).

FURTHER READING

ASHTON, T. S. (1955) *An economic history of England: The 18th century*, Methuen.

CHALONER, W. H. and MUSSON, A. E. (1963) *Industry and Technology: a visual history of modern Britain*, Studio Vista.

CHECKLAND, S. G. (1964) *The rise of Industrial Society in England 1815–1885*, Longman.

CLAPHAM, SIR J. H. (1930–8) *An economic history of modern Britain*, 3 vols., Cambridge University Press.

FLINN, M. W. (1966) *The origins of the Industrial Revolution*, Longman.

HARTWELL, R. M. (1967) (ed.) *The causes of the Industrial Revolution in England*, Methuen.

HOBSBAWM, E. J. (1968) *Industry and Empire*, Weidenfeld and Nicolson.

JONES, E. L. (1967) (ed.) *Agriculture and economic growth in England 1650–1815*, Methuen.

MANTOUX, P. (1961) *The Industrial Revolution of the 18th century*, Jonathan Cape.

MATHIAS, P. (1969) *The first industrial nation: an economic history of Britain 1700–1914*, Methuen.

ACKNOWLEDGEMENTS

Grateful acknowledgement is made to the following sources for illustration used in these units:

Aerofilms for Figures 2 and 3; S. Elliot Educational Films, Stoke-on-Trent for Figure 27, Lewis Textile Musem, Blackburn for Figure 18; Mansell Collection for Figures 4, 17, 19, 29 and 34; Pilkington Glass Musem, St. Helens for Figure 28; Science Musem, London for Figures 15, 20, 21, 22 and 35.

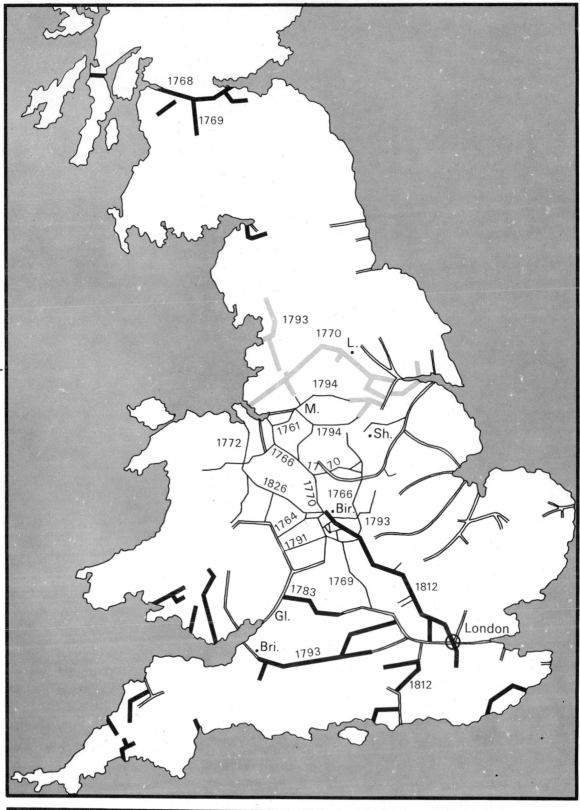

Canals and Navigable Rivers 1830   (with dimensions of locks)

| | Rivers | (Pre-1750) | Broad | 13x70 |
| | Narrow | (7'x70") | Northern | (40'x10") |

Dates of Authorisation of Canals Given

Figure 32

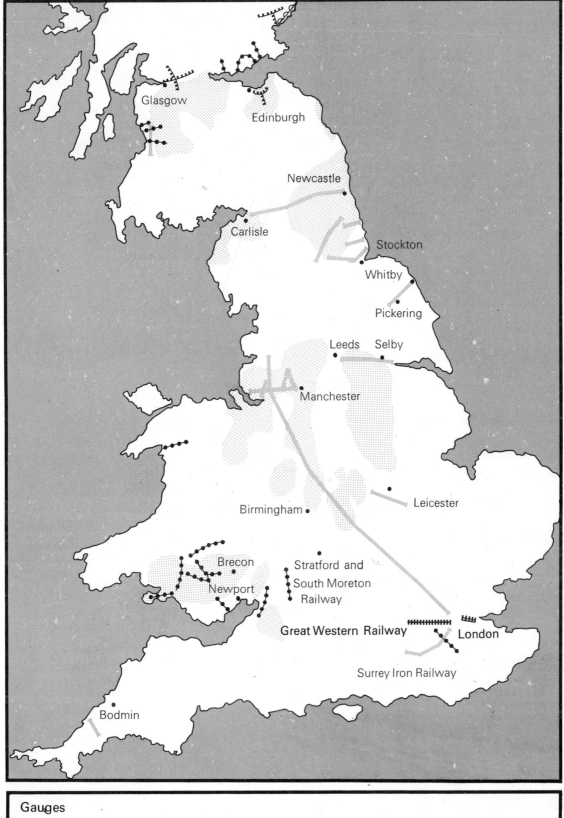

Railways in Britain Open in 1838

Gauges

••••••••	4'0" and less	....	4'6"	————	4'8½"
┼┼┼┼┼┼	5'0"	○○○○○○○	5'6"	┿┿┿┿┿┿	7'0"
░░░	Coalmines				

Figure 33

THE AGE OF REVOLUTIONS

A Study Guide to Stendhal's *Scarlet and Black*

An Atlantic–Democratic Revolution?

1 An Introduction
2 The 'Revolutions' before 1789
3 The Revolution in France
4 The 'Revolution' outside France

History

5 ⎫
6 ⎭ The Industrial Revolution

7 Napoleon
8 Restoration Europe

Jefferson

9 ⎫
10 ⎭ Jefferson

Literature

11 Rousseau
12 Goethe and *Faust*

13 ⎫
14 ⎭ Wordsworth

Philosophy

15 ⎫
16 ⎭ Kant's Copernican Revolution: Speculative Philosophy

17 ⎫
18 ⎭ Kant's Copernican Revolution: Moral Philosophy

History of Science

19 ⎫
20 ⎭ Sir Humphry Davy

Literature

21 ⎫
22 ⎭ William Blake

Art History

23 ⎫
24 ⎭ The Concept of High Art and the Reaction to it

Music

25 ⎫
26 ⎬ Beethoven
27 ⎭

Literature

28 Stendhal's *Scarlet and Black*

Art History

29 ⎫
30 ⎭ Art and Politics in France

Religion

31 ⎫
32 ⎭ The Religious Revival in England

Romanticism

33 ⎫
34 ⎭ Romanticism